JUMP NOW,
MRS WILLIAMS

A missionary memoir

Joan Williams

CONTENTS

TO THE READER

I was born in January 1936, just before the Second World War, and I learned to count by the bombs dropping on Liverpool. My parents were godly people and I was early taught my duty to God and those around me. Very early in my life I felt that I was 'special' and that God's hand was on me. I married a man whose sense of commitment and honour to God was preeminent in his life. We were blessed with two fine children who are still my pride and joy.

So much has happened during my life time, and I would like to invite anyone who reads this book to share some of the details of what I have been privileged to experience in my happy, sad, and God-blessed life.

During our years on the mission field the whole spectrum of service changed. When we went to Burma in 1960 there were 97 missionaries in the area. When I retired from active service in 1997 there were just 3 remaining.

Although I have been 'retired' for almost thirty years and 'alone' for over forty, I am still very aware of God's leading in my life. I wrote much of this book in the beautiful tranquillity of the house by the river Tavy which my father-in-law left me for my retirement; I completed it in the noise, the hustle, and the bustle of Calcutta, a City that I have grown to love above all others.

13/1/39. I.H.Q. POST CARD

My dear Joan,

    The General is sending
you this card on your
third birthday with her
love, and wishes you
many happy returns of
the day.

    The General does hope
you are keeping well, and
that you will have a jolly
time tomorrow.
     With love,
         L. Colonel.

Miss J.Wright,
27 Eccleshill Rd.
Liverpool, 13.

"THAT'S JESUS!"

CHAPTER ONE

THE LEAVING OF LIVERPOOL

1936-1960

CAPTAIN AND MRS. WRIGHT AND JOAN

Wartime beginnings: 1936-1944

One of my first memories is of helping my Mum and Dad deep down in the underground shelters under Liverpool, St George's Hall. My parents were Salvation Army Officers, stationed at their first Corps at Liverpool Knotty Ash, pictured in the photo on the previous page. The Salvation Army had been offered the warren of passages in order to house the people who had been bombed out of their homes. Bunk beds had been placed at both sides of the passages and the bomb-dazed people spent their days and nights there waiting for the bombing to cease. At intervals there were larger spaces which were quickly made into 'rooms' in which refreshments were distributed. Every morning my Mum and her helpers made sandwiches and put them into long wooden trays ready to give out in the evening to the people.

I remember my big strong Dad arriving with the trays and the people making way for him, and Mum 'clearing the decks' so that the food could be given out. My job was to squat on the counter right at the end where the tea was given out, and to distribute the crusts (with margarine on them) to teen-aged boys. Mum had said: 'When you see a big boy, let him have one extra crust'; so I knew this was my special job.

Once I was sitting on my Mum's knee in the underground air-raid shelter, having run down the steps when we heard the bombs dropping. We had to sit on long backless forms facing each other and just look into other scared faces as the noise howled around us. One lady just opposite us suddenly went berserk. She tried to hide under the seat and couldn't get low enough on the floor, so she sat down and screamed: 'They've taken my Dad and my husband is in France and now they're coming for me.' My Mum turned me round and hid my face in her dress, but I still remember the horror on that lady's face. When I looked again the few men around had taken the lady away to 'give her a cup of tea and help her calm down.'

Although Mum and Dad married in June of 1931, I was not born until January of 1936, and Mum had always told me that I was a 'wanted child.' Theirs was a hectic, busy life. One of the things they were asked to do was to provide soldiers who were leaving Liverpool Docks with a parcel of food. They were given three different kinds of sandwiches (spam, cheese, and powdered egg mixture),

a packet of Smith's Crisps, and a packet of biscuits. My job here was to sit on the counter of the mobile canteen and issue out five cigarettes to each man. The cigarette box was a large carton with a small hole at the base from which I scooped the five for every man. They would try to get another one from me saying, 'I've only got four, love', and I would always be very careful to see it was five and tell them so! In these instances, I early learned that in order to be happy yourself, you have to make other people happy.

During the war it was known that harmful gasses were part of the bombing plague that came over from Germany. Many children, myself included, suffered painful boils and carbuncles all over the body. These had to be dressed every other day and I remember dreading the sound of water being poured into the tin bath ready for me to soak off the dressings. My Mum used to gently ease the gauze off my sores and re-dress the wounds for another day. I was probably five or six at the time, but this is not a good memory. One day, a bomb dropped about three houses down the street from us. The lintel of the door frame in the main room where we were staying fell on my foot and smashed my little toe. It had to be removed, and I spent a good few months learning to walk on parallel bars. I am not sure just when it was but I went to stay for a while at Strawberry Fields – the Salvation Army Children's home made famous by the Beatles. The Officers there were kind, but other children picked on me because I had a Mum and Dad, who visited me every few days. They told me my parents would not come back, and I remember being so relieved when they visited again. Most of the children there were orphaned or of one parent families. I well remember the moment of complete silence when my Dad said: 'Come on, we're taking you with us to-day.' So many of the other children would have loved to have heard those words, and as my Dad lifted me from my little bed I remember feeling so special and loved.

Early in the war Mum and Dad had 'adopted' a young woman called Betty Drew, pictured here with me sitting on a table next to her. As a young child she had lived in a Barnardo's home along with her elder brother and sisters. She was the baby of the family, and her sister, Sadie, who was about eighteen years older,

and had become a Salvation Army Officer, took Betty out of the home as soon as she could. Betty then joined her sister's new family, but Sadie and her husband were appointed to go to Thika (in Kenya) in order to commence a Blind School. Because of this, at the age of sixteen, Betty came to live with us. She worked with Mum and Dad all through the War years, and then got her own flat in St John's Wood, and became a very well respected hospital receptionist.

One day when Mum, Dad, Betty Drew, and I were going into the house a doodle bug came overhead. When they stopped they dropped (as the war information folk used to say), and this one stopped just above us. Betty was trying to get the key in the lock so we could get in the house quickly, and we three were standing behind her. Dad said: 'Come on Betty, hurry up and open the door!' Just then the bomb dropped and the blast knocked Mum, Dad, and I flat on the floor. The blast then was fully on Betty. She was thrown right up the stairs of the house with her skirt over her shoulders and sprawled out in a very undignified way. Probably in fright more than anger she yelled at my Dad: 'Alright, there's no need to push!'

Dad used to drive the mobile canteen and sometimes I'd go out with him. I remember one time when the blast just got hold of the van, lifted it into the air, and placed it (quite gently) about twenty yards down the road. Many of the cups and saucers were broken, the tea urn lost its tap, and the tea was sloshing all over the floor but we were all safe – and the precious sandwiches were still intact! The other doodle-bug story I remember is that

Dad was asked to initiate a young officer called Denis Hunter (later to be Commissioner) into the Salvation Army work in Liverpool. They were walking down the main street and Dad explained about the doodle-bug bombs. At that time a doodle-bug flew over them and stopped. 'What do we do now?' said Denis Hunter: 'Pray?' 'No', said my Dad: 'Run!' At Mum and Dad's 50th wedding Anniversary many years later, then Commissioner Denis Hunter related this happening and said: 'I learned early on that Brigadier Wright was a man of prayer, but he was also a man of action.'

When we were at home (which was not very often) and the bombs dropped, we used to sit under the stairs and count the bombs coming. Mum pretended it was a game but I knew by the look on her face it was no game. One day we left the Salvation Army hall early to go home and during our short trip to the house Mum decided to go to a neighbour and ask if we could shelter with them, as the bombs had started before we got home. Our road was bombed and the house next to ours had what is termed 'a direct hit.' I vividly remember meeting up with Dad about four hours later and him saying to my Mum: 'I thought I'd lost you both.' He had heard our road had been hit and had been looking for us whilst we were sheltering in safety.

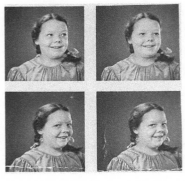

Soon after this I went to live in the Isle of Man with a friend in the Corps where Mum and Dad had served before the war. It was like another world and I remember wondering if a bomb had dropped on our house in Liverpool and I had been killed and was now in heaven. There were no bombs and no scared-looking people running around all day. Also people had time for each other and everything seemed to be happening in slow motion. I rolled boiled eggs down a hill of gorse at Easter. I fished from the sea wall with an 'uncle', and was allowed to grow my hair long for the first time in my life. I had been named Joan Margaret to be called Margaret but people called me Peggy, which horrified my Mother. I was therefore called Joan. I still do not know why, but I loved the name Gwendoline, and said it to myself at least ten times a day. When I arrived at the Isle of Man and was asked my name, I said 'Gwendoline', and that is what I was called the whole of my time there. I remember sitting in front of the mirror, brushing my hair, hoping it would grow longer, and saying to myself, over and over: 'Gwendoline.'

Many years later, when I was commissioned to be a Salvation Army Officer, the lady who had looked after me in the Isle of Man read about the fact in the War Cry. She travelled all the way to the Royal Albert Hall in London, just expecting to get a ticket. Of course it was fully booked. My Dad saw her, and gave her his ticket, much to my Mum's consternation. But he had a plan. Just before the meeting started and the Staff Band walked in, I noticed my Dad sat on the back row, holding an instrument he had 'borrowed' to get in.

When I was nearly seven, I went to Grays in Essex, to live with Aunty Lil, Uncle George, and their son John, whilst Mum and Dad continued their service in Liverpool. Aunty Lil had dearly longed for a girl, as she was a seamstress and just longing to make pretty dresses and hats. She had been told that she could not have any more children, so John was dressed in satin suits and patent shoes with velvet bows on, and I used to feel so sorry for him! Aunty tried to dress me in nice clothes but I preferred filling my dolls' pram with bricks and stones and enjoyed such 'boys' things as climbing trees. She quickly gave up on me. John used to stand under the tree I regularly climbed (he was nine months younger than me), and say: 'You're not supposed to do that', and I would reply: 'I know but I like it here – why don't you come up?' But he never did; he would have spoiled his suit. Once at a family wedding, John and I were the bridesmaid and page-boy. As we walked down the aisle, he whispered to me: 'One day, I'll marry you like this.' And I said: 'Ok'.

A life-long Salvationist, John served, together with his wife Davena, at Grays, Southend, and Hastings Ore, and he was principal euphonium player in the London North East Fellowship. In retirement, we became firm 'Facebook friends', and enjoyed each other's company whenever we met. Like my Dad in many ways, John was always well-loved by young people in particular, and his influence on many of the younger folk of the corps was obvious at his recent funeral. John never really recovered from losing his beloved Davena, and it is good to know that they are now together once again.

I remember Grandma Smith, who lived just round the corner from Aunty Lil, as a woman of prayer. She had been married, a mother and a widow by the age of twenty-one. She was my Dad's mother, but we called her 'Grandma Smith' because of her third and last husband, Ebenezer Smith. He lived with our family for a while after Grandma died; but he left to go and live with his daughter when I was about twelve years old. Aunty Florence Staines was Grandma's first child, from her first marriage; I had very little to do with Aunty Flo as a child, but later when we lived in Bath, at the Carfax Hotel, she came to visit now and then. I do remember that she became a Top Buyer in Selfridges.

After Grandma Smith's first husband died, the Officer at Grays Corps suggested that a farm hand from

Ockendon (a village nearby) should be her new husband – and so he became. Samuel Wright – my Grandpa – could neither read nor write, but Grandma taught him over the next few years, and he eventually became the well-respected Sergeant Major of Grays Corps. Their five children were Cecil, Percy, Ida, Wesley, and Lily. Very little is known of Ida as she left the home early. Percy was killed in a motor cycle accident before he was married. Lil was the youngest, and the eldest by eight years was Cecil, who became an Officer and was in the Salvation Army Assurance Society for most of his life. The middle child, my Dad, Wesley Samuel, an early and keen member of the Young People's Band (pictured here sitting on the front row, under the drum), grew up to be a 'Torchbearer' along with my mother in the 1933 session of Cadets.

Grandma Smith was so very proud of her two Officer sons and spent her life knitting black socks for their uniforms. She always felt the Army had made a mistake, as her opinion was that one son should have been the General, and the other the Chief of the Staff. For her part, Aunty Lil served in the Corps at Grays all her life. My Dad and his sister were close in age and so there was always a little friction in the home. The story is told regarding Dad doing his homework and asking Lil what the time was – as she was in the room where the grandfather clock was. She just said: 'I don't know, I can't see.' My Dad came into the room, put her face close as possible to the clock and said: 'Now what is the time?' Lil replied: 'I still can't see. I've got my eyes closed.' At this, my Dad pushed her face through the glass of the clock. A visit to the hospital was necessary for stitches to the wound.

Aunty Lil was responsible for my Mum and Dad meeting. Mum attended the Life Saving Guards (a girls' activity group similar to the Guides) at the Corps, and Lil suggested that Mum came home with her for tea. When Grandma Smith saw Mum she said: 'You're Pearl Green. Your Mum and Dad used to attend the meetings at the Corps, but left a few years ago.' My Mum knew nothing of this, but Grandma Smith remembered a photo of Mum's parents in uniform and showed her. The sad story was that they were good soldiers at the Corps but a young Captain at the Corps, knowing that Grandpa Green had a coal business, said: 'Mr Green, the Lord has told me that you will give me £100.00 for work in the Corps.' To this Grandpa Green replied: 'Well when the Lord tells me, I will give it to you, but until then, I will not be at the meetings.' He was so annoyed by the audacity of the Captain that he and his wife did not return. Later when my Mum felt she should become a soldier and wear uniform, Grandpa Green forbade her to have the uniform in the house, so Mum had to leave her uniform at my Dad's house and go there to change before going to the meetings. Later still when Mum and Dad went into Training, Grandpa Green was still further annoyed, and told them they were not welcome in his house. When he knew he was dying some years later, he did ask my Mum and Dad back to the house to pray with him, but he never returned to the Army. Grandma Smith was 'near death' several times. I can remember at least three occasions when we all squeezed into the horrible little car in Liverpool and rushed to make the long drive down to Grays (there were no Motorways then), only to find her cleaning windows or something similar, clearly fully recovered. On the last of these occasions, she was sitting up in bed, with a full plate of bacon and eggs on her lap, wondering why we'd come. She eventually died with a cold.

In August 1944 my sister Elizabeth Ann was born. My mother, still working in Liverpool, was walking in the park and slipped on some wet leaves. The baby was born at only 8 months old and weighed just 2 ¼ lbs. She was a month in hospital, and when she finally came home, I was so disappointed to know that I could not touch her, and I certainly could not hold her. She was still so ill and so fragile. I was willing to give her any or all

of my doll's clothes, but they were all too big! Special dresses and woollen clothes had to be made for her. Eight is not a good time to have a new brother or sister, particularly when you have been 'king pin' in the family. The baby seemed to moan all day and cry all night, and I felt like the whole of my Mum's attention was on her. Ann was always a sickly child and therefore needed special nursing care.

When she was seven (and I was nearly sixteen), she was diagnosed with Tuberculosis, and was so ill for three years. Mum and Dad were then stationed at Lincoln Citadel, and a half-night of prayer was held at the Citadel for her. We found out that Ann had also prayed, whilst in hospital that she would be home for her birthday – and really believed that this prayer would be granted. By this time, she was so ill that she had been released from hospital in order, the Doctor said: 'to make her comfortable before she goes, as there is nothing more we can do.' There is no doubt a healing was performed on her small body by the power of prayer. When the Doctor was re-visited a month later, he was almost annoyed by the improvement he saw in Ann. He said: 'I have been made to look foolish. I know that this time last month this child was full of T.B. Yet this month there is no sign of it. We have done three sets of X-rays, and can find no trace of it.' Ann went back to school, and never looked back.

Later in life, when she emigrated to Canada, a full body scan was necessary, and we wondered what the result would be. She had complete clearance, and was therefore able to start her new life over there. She raised two daughters more or less on her own, until she remarried the marvellous Ken Leach in the nineties. They visited Tavistock and Oxford several times, and shared many happy and adventurous years together, before Ann died, too early and too quickly, this last Spring. One of the unexpected comforts for both of us in her last days in the hospice was reading passages from this memoir and so recalling our shared early life together.

New horizons:
Bath, Lincoln, & Torquay, 1944-1955

A few months before the end of the war, we moved to Bath in Somerset, where I joined the Sunbeams at the Citadel (that's me in the middle of the group in the photo). Mum and Dad had been appointed to run the Red Shield work with servicemen. This was late 1944, the war had not yet finished, and around Bath were many military barracks: Melksham, Calne, and Trowbridge. These young men (and some young women) would be free at week-ends and came into Bath for a good time. There were few places for them to stay and the Army were given a series of prefabricated huts in which to house and feed them. There would be up to five hundred every Friday and Saturday night, and my Mum and Dad seemed to be constantly making sandwiches and soup for them. Dad used to concoct meals from the most unlikely things which had been given during the week, for sale at the week-end. I remember he was given 1,000 tins of pumpkin slices in brine. He went into the kitchen, spent a couple of hours with some sausage meat, seasoning and tomato sauce, and then on the menu that week-end (and the next two) were 'Savoury rissoles'; they went down a storm!

I vividly remember one Sunday morning when a special 'happening' occurred in the canteen (pictured here). The servicemen used to be keen to get the cooked breakfast provided and there was already quite a bit of jostling for position and noisy banter. Captain Anishka was a young Russian Officer sent to help my parents in the running of the canteen and her English was not good. This day she was a bit worried that the troops were getting out of hand. She stood on the counter and said: 'Now come on you B——rs, get in line!' They all cheered and quickly got into line but my poor Dad was aghast at the Captain, in full Army uniform, swearing at the men.

He immediately took her into the kitchen and reprimanded her, to which she replied: 'Well, that's what they say to each other', which, of course, was true.

Once the war ended, Dad was asked by the Salvation Army to look for a suitable hotel from which work with the servicemen could continue. The old prefabricated huts were to be pulled down by developers in the town. The Carfax Hotel in Pulteney Street which had formerly been three houses used by the Admiralty during the War was the chosen location. Pulteney Street was, and still is, the pride of the town with grand Georgian buildings both sides of the street, and was a very well sought-after area. Letters were seen in the local papers about being 'astonished and concerned' that the Salvation Army should be allowed to move in. What were they going to do with this centre, and would it not bring down the whole tenor of the area? But the Mayor of the day was very supportive, and said so in no uncertain terms. He made it known that he had given a substantial donation and expected 'great things' of the work to be done there.

Dad decided that the first two floors of the Hotel should still be for the usual Hotel guests, but that the top two floors should be for servicemen. Of course there were some guests who decided not to be in the same Hotel as servicemen, but there were also others who thought it a wonderful idea. To see tired and often exhausted young men and women arrive in uniform at the beginning of the week-end and later come down to the dining room spruced up for the occasion, looking thrilled to bits to be in a Hotel with friends, was quite something. Of course the service folk did not pay full Hotel fees, but the place still ran at a good profit.

One of the groups that my Dad had come to stay at the Carfax was the Amsterdam Concertgebouw orchestra and they took over the whole place as there were so many of them. It was during their stay that I learned the Dutch sense of humour was not the same as ours. They saw my Dad going to the Army meeting with his tenor horn. The leader then said to Dad: 'I want to introduce you to the finest horn player in the world.' To which Dad said: 'Well, you haven't heard me play yet.' The leader apologised profusely, and asked when they could hear Dad play. Dad replied that he only played for the Glory of God and usually in the Salvation Army Hall. They regretted that they did not have a night free to come to hear him play, and my Dad feigned disappointment. Dad's love of classical music was real, but he was self-taught. In his retirement he made a remarkable collection of tapes of all sorts of classical performances from the radio. I now feel that his love of classical music has been passed on to me; in my retirement and now that I live alone, the sound of the music of a wide range of composers has become increasingly important to me. There is usually music of some kind on in my house and, at times of illness I feel that Mozart, Chopin and Shostakovich know exactly how I feel and just what I need to hear.

During my days in Bath I was attending Oldfield Secondary School and enjoying life immensely. I was in the School Swimming Team and was soon chosen for the county team and later to swim for England. I specialised in the back-stroke and practised hard and long to improve my timings. I was also a keen and energetic water polo player and played for Bath City. I grew my nails long so I could scratch the opponents' backs, and became expert at pushing people underwater and then standing on their shoulders whilst I threw the ball! Along with this (for which I was praised by my team trainers), I was one of four pupils chosen to try to pass some General Certificate of Education examinations. Usually only the pupils at the local High School took these exams but they were the opening to so many opportunities in further education and it was thought that this 'experiment' should be tried at our school. We had an excellent form teacher in Miss Powell who encouraged us in every way. It was decided I should take English literature and General English language. For the next year the four of us stayed after main school in the evenings and took home homework every night. I found it fascinating and again, felt special. Given the rest of my general education, I felt I was doing especially well at English, and really enjoyed it, too. At the end of the year we travelled to Bristol University to take the examinations, and I was so grateful and happy when I passed both English literature and General English language with A grade marks. Three of us passed with good marks, the other did not, and was most distressed about the whole thing. I remember feeling so sorry for her because she had worked as hard as us and in many ways seemed very ready for the exams.

My social life at this age (around fifteen to seventeen) also blossomed. I had many and various boy-friends, much

to my mother's concern, and words of wisdom were dropped as often as possible. During this time also I was very aware that God was working in my heart and challenging me in ways I had never experienced before. Peter Ward was my first real boy-friend. Most of the boys who came to the Corps at Bath were from Army families, but Peter was different. He was the only one who attended from his family, and I admired the fact that he was so keen and so regularly at the Army. He was a bit of a mystery that I wanted to solve. The more I knew of him the more I liked him, and we would spend most Saturday afternoons together, walking in the hills around the lovely city of Bath. Our favourite walk was to a place called Sham Castle, where we would talk about anything and everything in general, and share our hopes for the future. I shared with him that I felt God was calling me to be an Officer and he was very honest and open and said: 'I could never do that – I really don't think it is within my make-up to be so public in my faith.' Looking back, I think I feel that I was slowly falling in love with Peter, but when I knew he felt he could not be an Officer I also knew that our friendship must finish. Of course I later married Railton, and Peter later married Jean Spencer, and together they became Officers, and very good ones at that. The call to Officership is a very clear and insistent one... Some time after Jean's tragic death, Peter married Brenda Tullock and they lived in retirement in Basingstoke. Peter himself died earlier this year after a long illness: another of my friends gone to Glory!

After Bath, Mum and Dad were appointed to Lincoln Citadel, since Dad had specifically asked to go back on the Field. But this was not without problems. I had to stay at the Goodwill centre in Bath to do my exams although Dad had asked the Army if they would delay the move for my sake, and the powers that be had responded by telling him to move three months earlier on disciplinary grounds. When I eventually joined Mum and Dad in Lincoln I went through a time of rebellion. As mentioned earlier, I loved swimming and the invitation came for me to swim in France for England on a Sunday. My Dad would not allow me to take part, and was surprised that I had even thought he would give his permission. I was very angry and decided that this was the last straw: if I could not go swimming on a Sunday I certainly would not attend the Army meetings. Mum cooked bacon, eggs and tomatoes on Sunday morning as it was a full day of service at the Army. For weeks I stayed in my bedroom – smelling the bacon (and so wanting it) but stubbornly refusing to go downstairs and be part of the usual Sunday. This nonsense continued for two years, and I finally attended the meetings again because

I was friendly with one of the bandsmen who kept calling at the house and asking me to go back to the Army.

Lincoln Corps was an important part of my social life. I was in the Songster group of the Corps which then became one of the best groups in the Division. The Songster Leader (Harry Whitwell) was strict but fair and we all respected his knowledge of music. It was at Lincoln that I began to pay attention my Dad's preaching and realised that he was quite interesting to listen to. I experienced the challenge of spiritual understanding and commitment and felt called to Officership once again. At first I could not believe I had been chosen for His special work, and was so frightened by the prospect that I held it in my heart. There were two main influences which made a difference to me.

First: whilst we were still in Bath (when I was around 16) I used to go visiting with a Lieutenant Joan Lockwood (later to become Major Padfield) from the Goodwill Centre. We went to see an old man whom we knew was dying. We washed him, made his bed with clean sheets, did the washing up, and made bread pudding with the stale bread we found in the cupboard. At the end of all of this he said: 'Before you go could you please get my pipe going? I haven't got the strength.' The Lieutenant took the pipe into the kitchen and gagging at least three times finally got it going. He died a few days later but the Lieutenant's act of sacrificial kindness was, to me, beyond the call of duty and I realised I wanted to be like her. Just recently, in June 2017 I was privileged to attend the Major's 90th birthday celebration, and we enjoyed another meeting after many years.

Second: when in Lincoln I was in charge of the Salvation Army Brownies (small Girl Guides). If the girls did not attend two weeks running, I used to visit them to ask questions. I visited a child one day and there was no answer at the front door. I went round the back of the house and she was sitting huddled on the back step. Her mother was in hospital and she was waiting for her Dad to come from work. It was cold and raining and she looked the picture of misery. When I asked the neighbours why they had not helped, their reply was: 'They are not a good family and we don't want to be associated with them.' So this child of seven was suffering physically and mentally because of her parents 'name', and although I was only seventeen I was saddened by the injustice of it all. I felt I should do something about it and I also felt that the Salvation Army was a good way of doing this.

For two years in Lincoln I worked in the Office of Ruston Bucyrus (a crankshaft engineering company) as the office junior. Suffice to say it was enlightening but boring. During this period, Dad was the Salvation Army visitor for Lincoln prison. Quite a few folk were brought home 'for the week-end' in order for Dad to arrange their travelling home and so on (there was not much state help given in those days to ex-prisoners). Because there was a man and a woman this particular week-end the man slept on a camp bed downstairs and the woman was given my room upstairs. I went on another camp bed in my Mum and Dad's room. This was the first and last time this happened. I was seventeen and quite fashion conscious at the time. When we got up for breakfast the next morning Lilian (I have never forgotten her name) was not around. She had left the house along with a large suitcase full of my clothes, the small amount of jewellery I had, along with the sheets and pillowcases!! Mum was furious and I was in tears, but Dad was philosophical and said she must have been desperate to do that. It was a long time before I got over that, and I wanted to strangle Lilian.

From Lincoln Mum and Dad were appointed to Torquay in Devon. It was a special posting for us from the Army as they knew that my sister Ann had been so ill, but it was still a big lift for my parents. Torquay was one of the largest Corps in the area with a big band, large Songster Brigade and fine Young People's Sections. In the summer the congregation would swell to treble its usual size because of visitors who came on holiday. After the morning meetings the whole Corps would go to Babbacombe Downs where a well-attended open-air would be held. After a rushed tea we would have the evening meeting and then the grand march! We would line up outside the hall: the Band at the front, the young people in the middle, and the Songsters at the back – for the long, proud, noisy march through the town. With three flags flying we would completely take over the whole street. The Police would be there to stop the traffic at various points to allow our free access, and holiday makers and local folk would follow us as we processed our way to a place called 'The Slipway.' This was a piece of land which went from the promenade to the sea and where we held our two hour open-air. Dad asked me to form a timbrel brigade, which rather threw the strict Bandmaster, but within three months he was so

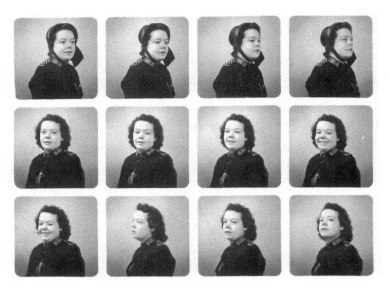

impressed with the playing, deportment, and obvious spectacle of the brigade that he invited us to head up the march. This had been a specially treasured duty of his band for years and I really admired the fact that his only thought was to get more folk to listen to the gospel, rather than keep his own importance.

Whilst in Torquay I was preparing myself to enter the Salvation Army Training College and so took part in many activities in and around the Corps to which I would not normally have been associated. My Father was aware of my feeling of uneasiness as far as Officership was concerned and one day told me the story of a Cadet who was in training with him. This young man had been in the church before coming to the Army and was a person who always used four words where one would have been adequate. One day, the training principal (Commissioner Hurren) asked if anyone would like to pray publicly. This young man rose to his feet and said in a loud voice: 'Oh thou ineffable God – Oh thou inestimable God – Oh thou omnipotent God...' to which Commissioner Hurren said: 'Oh, you unspeakable fool, sit down.' 'Remember', said my Dad: 'When you pray you must be sincere and be simple – those are the prayers God listens to.' I have tried never to forget that important advice.

'Leff Wright': Training College and after, 1955-58

I entered the Salvation Army International Training College for Officers in Camberwell in August 1955. My days there were not happy. Our session was one of the last nine-months sessions and I do not think I would have been able to undertake the two year sessions they now do. First of all, I was scared stiff of authority and frightened of doing the wrong thing at the wrong time. So much so that I now feel I was paralysed with fear

when I should have been listening to the teaching given. In many ways I was a 'girl from the sticks', having entered college from Torquay Corps. The girls (and boys) from London and around seemed far more with it and experienced, and I was intimidated by them. The first term was from August to December – when we were allowed home for the Christmas break. I decided that when I got home I would explain that training did not suit me and I could not go back. I would return to my old job as receptionist at the Kistor Hotel in Torquay, for my boss (Mr Jewell) had been sorry to see me go.

From the day I arrived home our lives were taken up with preparation for Christmas. There was the collection and distribution of food and toys for disadvantaged children and adults. Musical evenings celebrating Christmas in various venues followed and then, on Christmas Day, visiting the Hospital with the band. After the morning service we served a full turkey lunch for the lonely. Before I knew it I was getting ready to go back to college, facing the five months necessary before I could go out and do the practical work – my main calling and interest.

One of my clearest memories of my time in the Training College was when we as a group were asked to act out the story of Peter. I was very happy to have been chosen to be Peter in the rehearsal, but then came the time when he had to be thrown into prison. Our director, Major Fleur Booth, said to the guards: 'Much more aggression please. You must *throw* her across the stage.' When the time came for us to do the presentation, I was given a long satin dress to wear as a Peter's robe.

The platform where we did the drama had been scrubbed and polished, so when I was thrown into prison I went skidding at great pace across the face of the platform, and did not stop until I hit my head on a wooden post. I managed to get to my feet and to remember the few lines I was supposed to say. 'Wonderful acting' said Major Fleur Booth: 'You looked really quite dazed and confused' – I was!

I was very aware while in training that I was in some sense following in Mum and Dad's footsteps. But in the intervening twenty-five years, things had altered a lot. When Mum and Dad were in College, they were not allowed to walk together, since men and women had different pathways to go down. One day, Dad was seen crossing the lawn in order to give the key of their room to my mother. He was called into to Colonel (later General) Albert Orsborne, to give an account of this misdemeanour. He explained that Mum's lesson was finishing fifteen minutes earlier than his, so she would need the key first. He was told that this must never happen again, and he could now leave. As he did so, my Dad turned round and said: 'By the way, Colonel, I think you should know that I sleep with my wife!'

In college I was expected to conduct open-air meetings all by myself in a crowded market area, stand up at the front of a London Bus to give my testimony, and gather with a group of Cadets in a back street in Piccadilly where the prostitutes were soliciting. All of these things I felt to be both frightening and virtually impossible for me. But I did them. It was then every Cadet's duty to go Self-Denial Campaigning. This was a period of door-to-door collecting bringing in thousands of pounds for the Army's work. I was assigned to the commanding Officer and his wife (both Brigadiers) in High Wycombe. The Brigadier worked like a Trojan the whole time I was with them. His wife cooked and looked beautiful but nothing more. Every now and again he would say: 'How would you feel about coming with us to-day, dear?', knowing it would make such a difference to our daily total. To which she would reply: 'Well, I thought I would prepare home-made steak and kidney pie to-day, dear'. To this, he would say: 'Of course.' And that would be the end of the conversation. Our days were long: knocking on doors from 9 am–12 noon and again from 1pm–5pm; it was also cold and rather uninspiring. The houses were in a well-to-do area with most of the folk working at the nearby Pinewood Studios. I remember trudging along and wondering just how much more I could take. 50 years later I found myself unexpectedly driving down the Beaconsfield High Road. I remembered all the years that had passed since those training days. I was now retired, having been to places and seen things I could never have dreamed of then. I had been married, had children, and grandchildren, and was now driving my own car through the very street I had trudged through years ago as a young cadet. How blessed and special I felt.

The most important time of my stay at the college was Covenant day. We sang: *Mine to rise when Thou shalt call me,/ Lifelong though the journey be.* I meant it that day, and I always will try to adhere to that promise. Everyone thinks their session is the best, but our Sword Bearers session (also known as Dagger-Waggers) really was special. We had as sergeants folk like John Gowans (later to write the musicals and become General), Gisèle Bonhotal (later to be his wife), Joy Webb (of the Joystrings), and Daphne Parsons (later married to Will Hunter and friends with us in India and Pakistan). Fleur Booth was our House Officer, and Commissioner Frederick Coutts (later to be General) was our Principal. I was aware as I stood on the platform of the Royal Albert Hall for my Commissioning as an Officer that some cadets had been asked to leave as they were not deemed

THE DEDICATION, COMMISSIONING AND PAGEANT OF

THE 'SWORD BEARERS'

(1955–1956) SESSION OF CADETS

THE ROYAL ALBERT   FRIDAY, MAY 4, 1956

suitable for Officership. Some had left at Christmas (when I had thought of leaving myself) and not returned. Most of them were more able than I was in so many ways, and again I felt both special and aware of the tremendous responsibility of service now given to me.

My first appointment was to be with an 'old' Major in Morriston, South Wales. Doris Reading was a fine Officer who over the years had given many years of excellent service. As soon as she saw me she realised she had been in training with my Mum and Dad, so I was 'in'. The Corps was a good sized one with a Band of 40 and a Songster Brigade of 50. The Major made it her duty to always be the first at the hospital to see new babies,

OFFICER'S TRAVELLING INSTRUCTIONS

Name _____ WRIGHT _____

Date of Departure ___10th May 1956_____ *Leave T.C.* __10.30__

*Station*_____Paddington_____ *Time* __11.55 am__

*Book to*___Swansea_____ *Arrival* __4.15 pm__

Remarks ___Alight for Div. Welcome.
Bus to Morriston (2½ miles)_____

5M.
10.46

accidents, illnesses, and deaths. Many's the time we would have just prepared a hot meal and the phone would ring and we would leave everything and go. I still do not like congealed gravy on a plate. We did not have a car, and I also did not own a bike. I remember that my shoes were worn through by the November of that year. Major Reading was both a good speaker and a firm leader of meetings. I learned a great deal from her, but mostly I learned that 'to be available to the people' was of utmost importance. During my stay in Morriston we watched many nights as men who had worked in the coal mines struggled and then succumbed to phylicosis.

At another Corps nearby called Resolven was another young Officer called Railton Williams. He had been in training one year before me and had been known 'as a bit of a swot.' My Major obviously wanted to help things along and invited him (several times) for afternoon tea. Railton offered to help me with my lessons from the college – still necessary to complete before I was a fully commissioned Officer. This was the beginning of our courtship and marriage. Up until this time I had been friendly with Stanley Cleaves whom I had known from my days in the Corps at Bath. He was tall, good looking and had joined the Air-force. I thought he looked stunning in his uniform. He too had offered for Officership and had been in the same session as Railton. They had become friends in College and Railton had casually asked about 'the girl in the photo.' Once Stanley was commissioned and out of college he was in a wider world, and I soon found out that I was not his only girlfriend – he had quite a few. I felt let down and annoyed, but when I phoned my Dad to tell him his only reply was: 'I've been praying for this for the past two years – he's not the one for you.' This made me even more annoyed because in my heart I knew he was right, but I was not willing to admit it.

Soon after this, Railton wrote a lovely letter to me saying he had heard about our break-up and if ever I wanted a shoulder to cry on his was available. I was touched. One day whilst talking about the sort of partners we would look for Railton said, amongst other things he would want someone who could play the piano – he was hopeless at pitching a tune. (He had a good voice and when we were married and on the mission field we were often asked to sing duets together) Hearing this I decided that I would teach myself to play and so went for half an hour every morning to the hall and practised on the piano there. I could not – and still cannot – read music, but I can play many Army songs and choruses by ear, so that when, later, we became good friends and he asked if I could play I could answer: 'Well most things.' Now in my late retirement, I play the piano for Tavistock Corps and am known as one of the finest students of the Les Dawson Academy of Music!

After being with Major Reading for 18 months I was appointed in charge of my own Corps of Becontree in Essex. This was a small Corps with no band or songsters, but a huge Sunday school of 250 children. I had only four helpers and the children were not easy to handle. Most of them came from the huge Dagenham housing estate where their parents worked for the Ford Motor Works. They were little toughies and often we had fights in the hall. Whenever I walked down the street towards the hall, as they sat on the wall at the side of the road, with every step that I took, they would chant: 'Leff Wright, Leff Wright!' As I went quicker or slower, so would they...

One day the Divisional Commander and his wife were visiting and I decided we needed a bit more decorum in the Sunday school. I announced that those who came twenty minutes early would be given a sherbet dab. The usual 250 were there (with a few extras) and I then sat at the piano. We sang action songs, choruses – all needing the children to stand up, sit down, turn around, sing loudly and shout. By the time the DC arrived the children were so exhausted that they just sat and listened to all he had to say. 'You have wonderful control of the children,' he said. 'It cannot be easy with so many of them. Congratulations, Lieutenant!'

One of my memories of Becontree is having to clear away empty glass bottles before we could open the doors

on Sunday morning. On Saturday evening many of the folk living in the area would get drunk at a nearby Public House. Nearer still was a milk depot and empty bottles in crates were outside. Feeling skittish these drunk folk would smash the bottles against the front door and brick wall of the Salvation Army Hall. The resultant dribbled milk from the bottles and broken glass would be at the bottom of the wall and door. I usually filled four or five buckets with broken glass before being able to open up the hall for the Sunday meetings. It was not a good start to my day. The Corps closed about five years after my stay there, but I learned that people in small Corps work extremely hard and are incredibly loyal in every way. I felt honoured to lead them during my time there and was certainly sorry to leave the fine Sunday school.

During my time at Becontree, Railton and I were still courting and he would send me a letter every other day – sometimes of sixty-seven pages long. With an effort I could write nine pages but not often. Looking back, I wonder if Railton thought he was educating me (his schooling was certainly far superior to mine). He gave his opinions on world matters, the weather, the people in his Corps, and life in general. At the end of the letters, he usually said he loved me and always would, so it was worth reading through the first 66 pages. Although I admit that when we first became friendly I was a little hesitant, he completely won me over by his earnest sincerity regarding his Officership and his future work for God. By the time he asked me to marry him, I was convinced that we should be together for life.

In April 1957 I flew to Malta to meet Railton's parents.

his ticket is issued by B E A and accepted by the passenger subject to the Conditions of Contract (see page 2).

·BEA· is entered in the ·Via Carrier· box of Coupon(s). Any other entry in that box denotes carrier; details available on request.

you are unable to use your reservation, please let carrier now as soon as possible.

4. At most points in Europe, coach transport separately and you are advised to have the ap currency available.

tish European Airways is the actual carrier only when

DEPARTURE ARRANGEMENTS	COACH LEAVES AT	AIRF
Town Terminal Address		
Waterloo Air Terminal	2350 July 78 for	9 3
	LOCAL TIME	004
Phoenicia Hotel Valetta	1845 8 45 for	7 1
	LOCAL TIME	1930

IN GREAT BRITAIN— If joining at the Town Terminal you must be there NOT LATER THAN 15 MINUTES BEFORE COACH DEPARTURE TIME. If joining at the airport, you must check in NOT LATER THAN 30 MINUTES BEFORE THE AIRCRAFT DEPARTURE TIME shown on the FLIGHT COUPON — sufficient time should be allowed for this to be done.

OUTSIDE GREAT BRITA Check-In times vary so please locally for the time at wh must be at the TOWN TER or AIRPORT.

CK-IN
MES

E TO OBSERVE THESE TIMES WILL RESULT IN THE CARRIER'S FARE FORFEITURE RULES BEING

Mr Williams was in the Merchant Navy and he decoded messages from England and elsewhere. He and Mrs Williams had lived in Malta for quite a few years – as had Railton in his early years. They lived in an area called St Julien's Bay and arriving from Dagenham in Essex it was rather beautiful. The sea was a deep blue, the rocks were bleached white by the sun and the sky was seemingly low. Railton had not been told about my coming and the whole thing was arranged without his knowledge. His Dad said he had been asked to meet 'a visiting Salvation Army Officer' who was coming to the island and they were to look after this person during the stay in Malta. When I walked out of the terminus, Railton was rather underwhelmed by the situation, and said: 'What are you doing here?' I later learned that Mr. Williams loved surprises of any kind but would make so much fuss about it that most people would guess what was happening before it actually occurred – but everyone was supposed to keep on pretending!! Within four hours of arriving on the island we were at a place called Paradise

Bay and Railton had proposed to me.

In January 2014 I visited Paradise Bay again, while on a short holiday from my work at Bookworm Alley, the Salvation Army Bookshop and Resource centre which I set up in my retirement, in Railton's old family home in Tavistock. Paradise Bay was still a very beautiful place but very built up and commercialised. I sat at the place where I thought Railton had asked me to marry him, and I just thanked God for all the years that had followed that special day. It was on this holiday that I began to write this book.

When I was at Becontree Corps it was necessary for me to study in order to prepare my Sunday Sermons. At first I felt and told myself it was coincidental that I was increasingly drawn to the missionary journeys of Paul. I seemed to receive so much inspiration from them to share with my people on Sunday. Looking back, I now feel that God was preparing my heart for his special challenge. I visited my parents at Staines Corps. An Officer called Eunice Evans was on furlough from Africa and gave her testimony. For 12 years she had felt called to go to Africa as a teacher, but her mother was sick and she stayed in England because of this. When her mother died she went to Africa and the headmaster of the school where she was appointed said: 'For 12 years we have prayed that someone would come and lead us – and now you are here.' At the conclusion of the meeting I found myself half way down the aisle of the hall in an act of offering myself for missionary service, when I suddenly remembered that I was engaged to Railton and had not discussed it with him. My feeling was so strong that I promised God that day that even if Railton was not like-minded I would go where He wanted me to go.

Railton had been visiting his parents in Malta, and it was with some trepidation that I went to meet him at Heathrow Airport later in the week. I somehow knew I had to tell him about my calling before we left the airport building – worrying that this might well be the end of our friendship. Railton then told me that at the exact time I was kneeling in dedication he was looking over to the mainland from Malta and remembering the words of St Paul in his vision when he heard the words: 'Come over into Macedonia and help us.' He said: 'I don't know how you will feel about this, but I promised God I will go on the mission field and I cannot go back on that promise.' I believe that calling of Railton in Malta and me in Staines has been the special gift that sustained us in times of questioning. Again I thank God for His special dealing with us. When, after losing Railton, the Army asked me to return to India alone, I remembered my calling and felt happy to obey.

Marriage and the Call to the Mission-field: 1958-1960

On Saturday May 3rd 1958 I married Railton Louis Charles Williams. We had been told we could get married on or after May 3rd – the date of his 23rd birthday. This was the earliest 'permitted' age for Officer men, so Railton decided it would be on that very same day. The wedding itself was conducted by the then Field Secretary, Colonel Frederick Kiff. Betty Drew was my maid of honour, and

my sister Ann and my friend from College, Ann Mollett, herself later a missionary in Bolivia, were the two bridesmaids. Railton and I were both married in our Army Uniforms, but Mum had made a special effort with the flowers and I had blue irises, red roses, and yellow mimosa (the true Army colours) in my bouquet. It was Football Cup Final day and my Mum was worried that not enough bandsmen would be there for us to have a band for the service. Dad was sure they would all come to the wedding – and they all did.

The sadness was that Railton's parents did not join us for this day. An invitation had been sent but it was returned unopened – Mr Williams had decided that Railton was too young to be married, and had decreed that neither he nor his wife would attend the marriage. This is the first time I had seen Railton cry. He had secretly thought that their arrival would be another one of Mr Williams' last minute surprises – but he was

bitterly disappointed. My Dad drove us to the train station after the ceremony, and we made our way to Cliftonville in Kent for our honeymoon.

Our first appointment together was at West Norwood Corps in the South London Division. The hall was (and still is) on the main road into London and very much in the public eye. There was no money in the Corps but Railton and I decided we would spend our first month's salary buying paint in order to make the front of the hall more presentable. The railings (which were rusty) were rubbed and painted green and the front door varnished. Within a week we received an anonymous donation which was double the amount we had spent on the paint from someone who 'admired the work you have put in on the front of the hall.' It taught us an important lesson. If you go forward in faith God always makes sure the recompense follows. West Norwood was another small Corps, with just a few folk who gave valuable service to those around. There was something on every morning and afternoon and sometimes of an evening as well. We were attracting new people and again (like at Becontree) had a fine Sunday school. We won the cup for the best Home League in the Division at the Divisional Rally 1959 – not an easy task with Corps like Upper Norwood, Croydon, and Bromley in our area.

At this time there were many single ladies living in

flats in the huge Victorian houses which ran along the road into London. These women had been career women in London at a time when most women only desired marriage and a family. They were teachers, actresses, nannies and ladies' maids and all very independent beings and 'got together' people. We were often called to their homes in order to pick up unwanted items, and the resultant jumble sales we had with these things were well attended and snapped up by the folk who lived in the council tenements in the area. One lady has a special place in my memory. She had been Lady's Companion to several important people and had travelled the world looking after their every need. Afternoon tea in her home was wonderful with tiny sandwiches and huge cakes. I still have some of the dainty lace and embroidered doilies she gave to me then, and they have been with us in our travels around Burma, India, and Pakistan.

The late 1950s and early 1960s also saw many immigrants from the Caribbean coming to Britain to be drivers and conductors on the London Buses. Four Salvation Army young men came from Jamaica to our Corps and the impact was quite dramatic. They sang lustily (with lovely deep voices), prayed fervently, and just treated everyone as friends. A few of the old people were a bit non-plussed, but were soon won over. Because of their excellent voices we felt brave enough to conduct some outside open-air meetings and so attracted even more new people to the Corps.

In November 1959, Railton and I, together with Mum and Dad, attended a large Army meeting at Westminster

Central Hall in London (the Annual 'Day with God' meetings). General Kitching was appealing for people to go to other countries for service: 'There is a Corps in South America un-officered, a blind school in India with no one to lead them, and a boys' home in Burma who need officers. Who will go?' he said. Knowing that Railton and I had offered earlier in the year, but had been told to settle down to Corps work in England, my Dad mentioned this to the person next to him. An Officer sitting behind us pushed a piece of paper and a pen into his hand and said: 'Please put their names down on there.' He was Colonel Laurence Fletcher, and was Secretary for South Asia, and within a month we were called for an interview at International Headquarters and accepted for the mission field. We later learned that our Divisional Commander, aware of the fact that we had offered had blocked our application because he thought 'we were doing a good job at West Norwood and were needed more there than in Burma.' He was later disciplined regarding this.

Although we had already offered to go on the mission field 'wherever the need is greatest' as the Army form demanded, we had received no official reply and therefore took it for granted that our offer had been refused or forgotten. By February of 1960, I realised I was pregnant and was thrilled to bits. Railton and I had always said we would like three children. We didn't mind in what order they came but we felt we would like a complete family unit. My sister was 8 years younger than me and Railton's sister was 8 years older than him, and we both felt that we had been lonely children. Soon after confirmation of the pregnancy we attended the special meeting in London (mentioned earlier) where General Kitching was appealing for officers for the mission field. After I explained at the interview that I was now pregnant, it was decided that we would leave West Norwood Corps and go to the apparently much smaller corps at Sevenoaks in Kent. We were disappointed in that things were really happening in the West Norwood Corps. We then had a small band, a Songster brigade and a very alive young people's Corps, but obeying orders we left with heavy hearts, whilst also glad to know that the growth continued after we left. We later found several of the Corps members at West Norwood to be loyal and generous supporters of our work in Burma. Both Railton and I worked hard and long in an effort to make our quarters look warm and inviting for the new people who were to follow us. I was now five months pregnant but still managed to scrub the lovely marble tiles which ran along the long passage to our entrance hall into the flat. We polished the furniture, cleaned the heavy curtains and even managed to lift the huge carpet and drag it into the garden to be beaten. The place looked lovely.

When we got to Sevenoaks we were so disappointed. The paint on the front door was blistering, the furniture was piled up in one heap with the carpet over it – and the whole house smelt musty. The Corps folk then told us that the last officer had left the Corps in 'a bit of a mess six months ago.' This meant we had to start all over again with our cleaning regime (I shall never forget the state of the gas cooker). Sevenoaks 'Old House' – an awful name – was a home where fifty retired officers were cared for. The staff comprised of eight officers of varying ages, qualifications and characters but all very dedicated and patient with the older officers. Because these folk made up the bulk of the Corps we were invited every Tuesday to have 'high tea' with the staff. The Brigadier (in charge) sat at the head of the table and then the other officers would be in age and rank down to the newest and youngest lieutenant at the end. We were always offered pride of place – one on each side of the Brigadier. The general conversation would be about the well-being or otherwise of the officers in the home. One day the complaint was that a Mrs Colonel always insisted on having rice pudding after her main meal no matter what the other folk had. She insisted on this luxury every day, and the younger officers said it would not always be easy to deliver this demand. Not long after this Mrs Colonel was talking to Railton about us going on the mission field and about the fact that we were going to Burma. She said: 'I understand that there is a lot of blindness in India and Burma – I have a friend who worked in an Army blind school in India.' Quick as a flash Railton replied: 'Yes Colonel quite right – and did you know that their staple diet is rice?' She decided the next day to go with the normal menu for pudding and never again asked for rice. The staff were grateful for this intervention.

Many of the officers there had been real personalities in their earlier days. They had been pioneers of the work in many different countries and had worked hard and long in the service of God and the Army. Now in their older years they were frustrated by the limitations of the body – and probably by the lack of importance and responsibility which they had once enjoyed. I well remember one old Colonel who now could not now read but sat on the papers every day so that others could not read them. When he got up from his chair there was always a rush by others to see if the papers could be found. Another old Brigadier who had worked for years in Africa was completely blind and so handicapped by this fact. His wife had already died and he was always so sad looking. His hearing, however, was excellent and he could hear things that were said a long way away. He had been the Training Principal in three difference Colleges in Africa and it showed. He would listen intently to all that was said in the sermons on Sunday, and either say 'Hallelujah – Yes I believe it,' or 'No, not true – prove it!' Both Railton and I found it very off- putting, but it was good training for us as it made us very careful in what we said, and we checked our facts before preaching... The retired officers of Sevenoaks were wonderful old people and we enjoyed our visits with them. When we received our appointment to Burma, together with our sailing date they were most interested and encouraging. It felt as if we had lots of grandmas and grandpas urging us on.

Our daughter Janet Ann was born on September 8th 1960 at the Salvation Army Mothers' Hospital in Clapton, East London. Not an easy birth by any means. All I can remember is that after 48 hours of labour she needed high forceps to help her into the world. She was a big baby and weighed 9 lbs and 14 oz, but I was not allowed to see her for four days which worried me. I had twenty-four stitches and was sore for weeks afterwards.

This meant I did not go back to Sevenoaks to help Railton pack our things as it was decided that I should stay in Norbury with Mum and Dad. I felt sorry for Railton having to go it alone but I knew the house was far better than when we had arrived there. We knew we had only six weeks before we were to sail to Burma and, for my Mum and Dad these days were precious. Janet was their first grandchild and they doted on her every move. They would both sit for hours just gazing at her and saying how wonderful she was. They took turns in holding her and talking baby gibberish, but she was not really old enough to appreciate any of it.

One day when Mum and I were doing the washing up after a meal my Dad said: 'Come here and look! She just smiled at me.' My Mum, who was secretly quite peeved by this happening, said to me: 'It was only wind. Babies of three weeks' old don't recognise anyone and they certainly don't smile.' Dad was convinced otherwise.

Looking back, I realise that the sacrifice of our leaving England and going to Burma was a big one for them. We had been in the area all of our married life and often 'gone home' for a Sunday night fry up after our long days at the Corps. They were also always there for us to talk things over regarding the planning for our Corps and their past experience was invaluable to us. In many ways my Dad looked upon Railton as a true son, and was so proud of us both. When the baby arrived she was the icing on the cake – only for us all to go. When the day came for us to leave England we all travelled by train to Liverpool, from where we would set sail for Rangoon; it was a long, sad journey.

My husband was the light of his Mum's life and the fact that we were leaving England was, for her, an extremely sad happening. Her daughter Audrey, eight years older than Railton, also very special to her, was now estranged from her parents and Grandma Williams rarely saw her or her children. Audrey and her husband, a serviceman, had been posted to Singapore, so with our leaving England it meant that both of her children were now in another land. I always look on this as the reason why Railton's Mum and Dad (pictured on the previous page) first came to see us in Norbury, and then travelled up to Liverpool docks to see us off. For this auspicious occasion, Mr Williams decided he would give us a 1960 ha'penny for the baby: one of his surprises.

My Mum was also upset about us leaving, but very proud. My Dad was his usual ebullient self, trying to keep everyone upbeat and happy, but the general mood was not good. When it finally came time to say our 'Goodbyes' Mum said 'When I go down the plank of the ship I will not look back.' I know this was a dreaded moment for her but she was true to her word. Dad turned several times to wave, but she resolutely kept walking. We knew our term was seven years, and this was in the days of difficult correspondence and virtually no telephone conversation – and certainly no e-mails. We were back in Liverpool, but I was leaving for the mission-field, and I have a feeling Mum thought she may never see me again.

The next time I spoke to my Mum and Dad was Christmas 1962 – two years later. Railton had arranged a special telephone call for my Christmas treat. Christopher was now overdue but in order to take this phone call I had to travel into Rangoon, wait at the telephone building and be in line with ten other people who were to have calls that day. When my turn finally came I was so overcome and emotionally overcharged that I cried; my Mum cried, too, and finally the two men – Dad and Railton – took the phone call!

CHAPTER TWO

BURMESE DAYS

1960-66

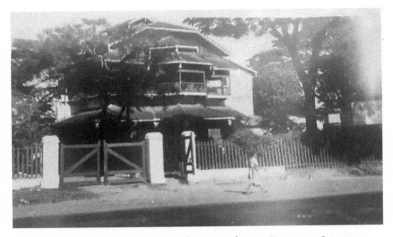

I shall never forget our first night in Burma. Janet was nine weeks old and had been quite sick with dysentery on the boat. Our kitchen was primitive. No gas, no electricity, no running water. I stood in the kitchen and thought: 'If my Mum could see me now.' In order to make Janet's bottle, I had to blow on straw to make a light and so get the fire going in a little hole in the wall. I then had to boil the water, before I could make her bottle – and by then she was both hungry and angry! Although we put a mosquito net around her she was red and raw with bites within two days, and it worried me so much. Our quarters was three rooms of the top floor of a big house (pictured here). The eighty boys lived downstairs and in two dormitories in the grounds. Major Rene Hammond, Captain Khin Than Aye, and Railton, Janet, and I lived on the top floor. There was also an office for the Boys' Home and an office for the Tamwe Corps – all on that one floor! The partitions started two feet off the floor and only went up to a height of eight feet. This meant that everything that was going on in the next 'flat' could be heard by everyone!! Major Hammond used to say: 'The baby had a bad night last night didn't she?' –meaning that we had ALL had a bad night! There was no privacy and very little dignity to our living accommodation.

The compound on which we lived was a large one. In one corner was a maternity unit which housed just eight beds, and this was staffed by a qualified midwife and her helper. The whole of one side of the square was comprised of the Boys' Home, which was a large two-storied building, with verandahs around the whole thing. It had multiple rooms which were used for all sorts of purposes. There was a beautiful large staircase from the front entrance to the first floor. It really was quite imposing and was used during the Second World War by the Japanese for their military officers. However, there was no running water and, no electricity and the toilet facilities were very primitive. The other two sides of the compound housed the Salvation Army Corps Hall building and the school buildings. We had a kindergarten and classrooms for classes up to eighth standard.

With eighty boys, a kindergarten class and a maternity ward as well as a Corps, we were always busy. I remember feeling constantly hot and tired and far from home. We did not have a refrigerator, and so had to be very careful as far as buying and eating food the same day was concerned. Once a month, as a special treat, we would go into Rangoon (a bus journey of three quarters of an hour) to a place called Queen's Hotel, and order a piece of ice-cold cake and coffee. During one of our trips on the bus into Rangoon, I realized I had been bitten high on my arm. Because I had my uniform on (which was up to the neck and with long sleeves) I tried to get at the 'thing' through my sleeve. However, I soon felt quite overheated and ill, and told Railton so. As I stood up, a scorpion fell from my dress. I have never seen a bus empty so quickly. People were jumping out of the window – handing their children to folk already out of the bus, and causing general mayhem in their effort to get away. By the time I got to the hospital my arm was about three times its normal size; my dress had to be cut away, my arm was raised and packed in ice, and there I stayed for four days, feeling very ill and extremely sore.

When Janet was six months old a baby boy was left on the steps of the Girls' Home nearby. Maung Kyaw Thein was a small sickly child, wrapped in a blanket, and left by his single mother, with a note on his vest which said: 'I give my child to the Salvation Army. Please look after him – he is ill.' He used to spend two days and nights a week at our house, being cared for, and playing with Janet and the boys in the home; the other days of the week he would stay at the Girls' Home. On consultation, we found out that he had a hole in the heart – the operation needed to deal with this could not then be performed in Burma. So Railton arranged for the Salvation Army to bring him to England, where a top surgeon at St Bartholemew's hospital performed the necessary operation. This case gained a great deal of media attention, and was in the main tabloids. Many couples offered to adopt Maung Kyaw Thein, and in the end a couple were chosen. The husband was himself a British heart specialist, and the wife was Burmese. When he was 21 years of age, he visited the Salvation Army International Headquarters, saw my husband, and offered to run the London Marathon for the Salvation Army that year – raising over £4,000.

Sometimes we were so tired from the day's happenings that I would wake up in the middle of the night half dressed – having fallen asleep in the middle of undressing myself! I also well remember getting Janet out to go to the loo, putting her on the seat, and then sitting on the bed to wait until she had finished. When I woke the next morning (probably three hours later), she had also fallen asleep and fallen down the pan! Just her head and little hands were sticking over the rim of the loo, and I was a long time getting over the shock and the guilt of that moment. At this time, I wondered why Janet always held her ears when she went to sleep, but nothing would convince her not to do it. Then I heard Indra, who helped in the house, saying to her: 'If you don't go to sleep quickly the bats will bite your ears' (they used to live in the roof of our house). I was really cross, but at least I knew the reason for the ear-holding.

In spite of all the difficulties we had, Railton and I were both very happy and fulfilled in Rangoon. We knew there was a work to do and we were glad to have the opportunity to be there and do it. We were seeing new people come to the services, and our singing group and band were improving weekly. Railton was not really a bandmaster, but he soon became one. I was not very good on the piano, but I soon learned new Burmese tunes, and also taught the interested young people how to the play the timbrel. The girls from the Salvation

Army Girls' Home joined with us for all of the activities, and we were aware of several friendships developing around us. The Girls' Home was about a mile away, and to see them all (around 70 girls) snaking down the main road of the village in their best clothes on a Sunday morning was quite moving. Our hall was a reasonable size, but folk had to come early in order to get a seat. Others who were late stood at the back or looked through the open windows. Our meetings were hot, noisy and at times raucous, but many important decisions were made during our quiet times, and from those children, nine later became officers in the work.

Our first day at the school was interesting. All the children would stand in the compound in class order and morning prayers would be said and sung from there. Our predecessor was Irish (Major Maud Dougan) and they had been used to her English language for years. So when Railton said: 'Good morning children', back came the reply: 'Good maarrning, Sir', with a strong Irish accent on the word 'morning'

Railton was one day informed that there was a young Chinese man who had already served five years in prison, but who had no hope of being released. He had been arrested on a small fraudulent matter (never proven), but his file had been lost, so he could not be tried. Several Chinese people came to ask Railton if he could help, and Railton made a suggestion to the authorities. If a file could be produced, could the man then be tried? The answer was: 'Yes.' So Railton made a very official looking file, with photographs and as much legal language as he knew, and then gave the file to the authorities. The case was then tried, and the man found not guilty. He was released from prison the same day and there was much rejoicing. His mother, known as 'Aunty Bo Bo', owned a bucket factory nearby, and on the anniversary of his release every year, she would give a huge meal (which included my favourite, *Khao shwe*) for the boys and girls of both homes as a 'thank you.' It was at one of these parties that Railton and I ate tiger (not knowing what it was). It tasted very much like pork, and was a white meat. It was only when we asked what it was that we knew.

At a school dinner in Tamwe, Railton and I also ate rats. There were two curries – one of chicken and the other of field rats. We decided to have the chicken and it was very good. When we were offered a second helping we both readily agreed. When our plates were retuned, mine had a tail in it and everyone knows that chickens don't have tails. The second helping was not as good as the first. Whilst Janet was still small I had a really bad encounter with a rat. The roof of our house was very high and gabled and all sorts of things lived up there – particularly rats and bats. The Burmese folk would often give Janet peanuts and *jaggery* as they knew she liked it. Sometimes she had more than enough, and out would come my handkerchief to 'get rid' of the extra piece. This had happened one day and I had then put the handkerchief under my pillow before going to sleep, forgetting the toffee was still in the corner. During the night I felt movement under my pillow, put my hand there and was bitten by a rat! This meant that I had to have seven daily injections of anti-tetanus injections directly into the muscles of my stomach – and I had the awful dread of knowing I might have contracted rabies until the month was over.

When I was six months pregnant with Christopher a new baby boy was born to officers on the compound. I was very interested as to how things had gone, and went to visit. Upon entering the house, I was told: 'The child will not live – he is not normal.' He was chubby and active, but his face was terribly distorted. He had a hare lip which extended right up to his nose. Because of this fact it was deemed the 'right thing' to not feed him and just allow him to die. I was most upset and tried to plead with the parents to look after him. When I protested hard and long, my husband was called to take me away. Later, the mother tried to convince me that it was best for the child and also for the other members of the family, as he would have been a constant responsibility for them all – but it unsettled me for quite a while.

Christopher was born in January of 1963 and Janet was so happy. First of all, when I told her that she was going to have a brother or sister for Christmas, but not

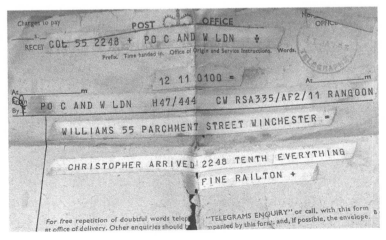

to tell anybody else, she said: 'Does Daddy know?' She then worried that, as the only children she saw were Burmese, there was a strong possibility that I might have a Burmese baby! At least four times she said: 'Will the baby be like me or like all the other new babies we go to visit?' When Christopher was eventually born, she was so proud and used to say to anyone passing: 'Come and look at our new baby – it's a boy AND he's English!'

When Christopher was just three months old and I was still breast feeding, I travelled to a new opening of a Corps. There was no hall and the service was conducted under a banyan tree in the middle of the village. Railton was not with me as he was conducting the Tamwe meeting so I was being accompanied by some National officers. Before the meeting started I felt that Christopher needed a feed as we had travelled three hours (on a bullock cart) to get there. I saw a Komodo lizard striding up the path towards the gathering and thought nothing of it, except that  it seemed interested in the people and was coming straight towards us. Suddenly I was covered by a blanket and several people tried to sit on me and on the outside of the blanket. There was great confusion and for a moment I thought I had been kidnapped. I was very uncomfortable and sweaty and really frightened. Then one of the Officers explained to me that I must stay there whilst they got rid of the lizard. Evidently this animal had smelled my milk and was wanting to drink, and the officers were aware of the situation that it would attack me – and Christopher if necessary to get the milk. I was almost more frightened afterwards than I was before, and was always very anxious to see that there were no lizards around when Christopher was still young and still breast feeding.

At Christmas we used to get parcels from America for the boys and there was always great excitement to open the 'used clothing' bales for them. One year my Mum and Dad sent a lovely blue lace dress and I put it in the usual parcel for the boys so that Janet would feel part of the scene. It didn't quite work like that as she had already worked out that the bales were only for the boys. When the lovely lace dress came out Janet said: 'Oh Mummy what lucky little girl is that for?' When I said: 'It is for you from Grandma in England,' she couldn't believe us because it came from the 'boys' bales' We then parcelled it up and put English stamps on it and had it delivered at the front door – only then could she believe it was for her. The boys called Janet Ma Sa Su – meaning Miss Nosey. She would squat down with them when they were talking (understanding Burmese completely) and then come and tell us all the stories she had heard about certain boys! They called Christopher Mr Iron-head as his head always looked bigger than the rest of him and when he fell over his head reached the ground first! I was aware that Christopher did not like Sunday mornings and he made sure everybody knew it too. The routine was that I would sit on the platform and Christopher would sit on the front row with one of the girls. If he was naughty, I would come off the platform, take his hand, and walk him out of the hall. All the way up the long aisle of the hall he would talk to people and say: 'I'm going to have a smack,' making me feel a real ogre. As well as this he would say when I smacked him: 'Didn't hurt – do it again.' I early learned that he was a mischievous and determined little boy, and far more difficult to control than Janet had been.

A man used to come and do banana fritters for our tea. He had a small petrol stove which he primed and set up just outside of the compound. Then he would make his batter from besan and pulse flour with jaggery. Once the fire was going he would put on his small wok like dish full of peanut oil, slice a banana length-wise in half, dip it into the batter and then place it in the boiling oil. Janet and Christopher would squat and watch the whole thing from start to finish. Having finished four bananas (eight pieces) he would sprinkle it all with sugar and hand it round to us. The whole thing took about 15 minutes but was very special and enjoyable.

When Railton was in charge of the school he was aware that one teacher was not willing to come to the morning prayers at the school and was also strongly Buddhist in his beliefs. This man openly ridiculed the Christian teachers in the school and, as he was a teacher for the older pupils, this had quite an effect on the general spirit of the school. Railton asked him to leave – and even arranged a better job in another school – but he would not go. Railton then asked the teacher to change his attitude and be more

accepting of other people's beliefs – he refused. Finally, Railton explained that the man would have to go and there was a great outburst of shouting and threatening from this man. All the teachers then told him he must go as he had 'shamed' Railton – which was a terrible thing in their eyes. He went and we thought it was all over. But he had paid some Knats (people who profess to be possessed by evil spirits) to 'give us trouble'. Very strange noises were heard in the classrooms at night and heavy desks – made of wood with iron frames – were thrown the other side of the class room, with seemingly no one around! Railton was walking the compound one night and a man stepped out of a bush and tried to stab him in the stomach (and Railton always had the scar on his third finger where he had saved himself and pushed the knife away just in time). This was an extremely frightening time for us – and our boys and we finally felt we had to exorcise the spirits. Railton used the words in the Bible and asked the evil spirits to 'Depart from this place', and after that we heard and experienced nothing more.

Ko Ko Gyi was a very naughty, cheeky but personable young man who won the heart of most folk who knew him. I do believe that he tried to be good, but found it very difficult. He came from a nomadic tribe in upper Burma, and although someone had brought him to the home because he was orphaned, it was not the place for him. He excelled at school, was very popular with other students, and showed real leadership qualities; but every so often he would run away, hitch lifts on trains and buses, and be brought back by the police. When he returned be would be very dirty, very hungry, and very repentant. But we all knew he would do it again within a few months. I often wonder what happened to him in later life.

Myint Tun was a very open-faced boy who was very popular with the girls as he was good looking and very pleasant to everyone. He was an excellent gymnast and was always at the top of the tower when the boys performed pyramids. He played *chinlone* (a game played standing in a circle – with a circular ball made of woven bamboo) to a high standard and was in the school team and the area team. He had no parents and no siblings, and was very much alone in the world, but was a very adjusted and happy young man. He joined the military and later became an 'underground spy' for the country. I could well imagine him doing this as he seemingly had no fear.

Maung Gyi came to us at aged 11 having lived much of his life with his grandma. They sold bananas and his job was to carry the large stem on which the bananas grew, so that when someone wanted to buy he would take the stem from his shoulders put it on the ground, and the buyer could pick his banana straight from the tree. Although now 11 years of age, he had never been to school, so started his days of education behind a kindergarten desk – with his knees sticking up above the desk as he was so tall. Railton promised him that as he worked hard, he would be promoted to the next class as soon as he was ready. He worked very hard. When it was time for football or *chinlone*, Railton would search and find him still studying. Then we realized he did not know how to play – this had never been part of his young life. Within three years, he was up to the correct group for his age – quite a wonderful achievement. Twice a year the boys had an opportunity to go home to visit relatives or friends. By this time, Maung Gyi's grandma had died, and he went to stay with his mother. He was then 14, and when he returned to the home asked for a special interview with Railton. He now realised that the reason he had been living with his grandma for so long was that his mother was a prostitute. He said he never wanted to go home again, and cried bitterly and was so ashamed of the whole situation. Railton was always ready to say that there were walls to be painted or classrooms to change when the holidays came, so that Maung Gyi could say he was 'needed at the home'. I understand that he now owns a brick factory, and has a family of his own.

Putoo was a very undersized boy, one of three children from the same family, who all came to the Army homes at the same time. I used to mix a glass of UNICEF milk for him every evening. He had a very winning smile and was thrilled to be singled out for special attention.

When, many years later, Railton and I visited Rangoon again, so as to conduct the Commissioning of the cadets from that year, Putoo met us at the airport. He now owned his own taxi, and had come to the airport to take us to the Home and I recognised his smile. The UNICEF milk had done the trick – he is now a big man.

Maung Gyi Lyn was an undersized child who came to us looking only half of his eight years. He needed special attention in that he was full of boils and I had to dress his wounds every morning and evening. Probably because of this, he would stand next to me at prayers every morning, and hold my hand. He came to us in November and was soon part of the Christmas preparations. During December he joined in all the usual parties and present giving, and was thrilled to know that his name was always on one of the parcels. Soon after Christmas when we were having morning prayers and all saying the Lord's Prayer, I overheard his version of the second sentence. Instead of saying 'Hallowed be Thy name', Maung Gyi Lyn had said: 'Our Father which art in heaven – how did you know my name?' I have never forgotten that morning.

Clarey Wallace was one of what we called 'the bigger boys.' He was from an Anglo-Burmese family and his sister Clara was at the girls' home. His English was excellent and he often translated for us. He had a certain steady charm about him and I always felt safe and assured when he was around. He married by far the most beautiful girl in the girls' home (and he was just one of her many admirers). They became Officers and did a good work, but unfortunately there was a clash of opinions with another Officer, and they resigned. Clarey now teaches the children of military officers.

Ba Shein was another boy who always used to stand near me at prayers. He was very bright and was usually smiling. He did well at school but was also quite naughty and was usually the leader if any mischief was around. At age 14, he wrote a letter to Railton apologising for all the trouble he had caused, and he promised to be a better person in future days. He completely changed from that day, and soon afterwards set his mind on studying to become an Officer. After training, he married had children and quickly became known as a pioneer and leader. He had a truly evangelical longing and was very keen on expanding the Army work. He used to travel miles to preach the gospel. He died early as the result of a heart attack whilst working in Upper Burma – where the main Army work now is. When he had heard of Railton's own untimely death, he said: 'I have lost the only father I ever knew.'

Kyaw Yin was tall and gangly for his age and always

demanded (and got) obedience from all around him. He also had a temper and would often 'fly' for no reason at all. When he was about 15 he asked for a private interview with Railton. He had a younger brother in the home but wanted to know if he had any known parents or other relatives. The answer had to be 'no' and he was visibly upset for days. Many of the boys were quite content when they were young and unaware of their situation, but when in their teens life became more serious and there were lots of questions to be asked and answered. To most the question 'do I belong to anybody?' had to be 'Not that we know of.' About two months later in a testimony period Kyaw Yin got up and sang in his lovely deep voice: *Now I belong to Jesus – Jesus belongs to me./ Not for the years of time alone, / But for eternity.*

Kyaw Yin married **Dora Aarons** (an Anglo-Indian girl from the girls' home). She was able to tame him somewhat. He joined the Burmese Air Force and was chosen to go to the USA for leadership training. He then

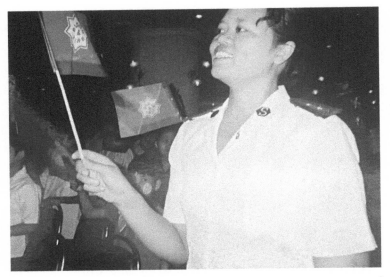

became an officer and he and Dora gave many years of faithful service in some very difficult appointments. Dora died early as a result of complications from diabetes. Kyaw Yin now lives in retirement with one of his sons. When I visited Rangoon for the 90th anniversary celebrations of the Army's work in Burma, I met Kyaw Yin and Dora's beautiful daughter, pictured here – the image of her mother. She is an officer and serving in Upper Burma.

As a child **James Aaron** was rebellious and naughty. He was the youngest of three children who had all come to the homes at the same time, and were now in the care of the Army. We felt he had probably been spoiled before coming to the home. At an early age it was obvious that he was a leader – and a popular one too. He was not satisfied with the boys' diet, and used to organize crow raids. The crows were caught, killed, and fried on campfires made at the back of the dormitories. Janet was violently sick one day and after being questioned said:

'Well I like fried crow'. When I heard this I knew where the crow had come from. When James was about twelve years old, he was one of about four boys who brought back to the compound a beautiful Pekinese dog. We felt it must have come from a good home, and soon knew that it belonged to a well-to-do Chinese family down the road. Evidently the gardener had seen the boys tempting the dog outside the fence with biscuits. Once outside, they all pounced on him and brought him home! Their story was that he had been wandering down the road and looked lost! James and his wife later became Officers, and were eventually appointed Command Leaders of Burma. They worked hard and saw the Army grow; now retired, they live with their family members.

One minor detail from this time which I remember as it was so important for me personally was regarding the mattress. In Burma there were no mattresses or soft quilting for beds. Probably because of the heat, all bedding was plaited bamboo mats on wooden bedsteads. About four months into my pregnancy with Christopher, I really longed for a soft bed. I put pillows on my back and front, but it did not really help and was not the same as a mattress. An American friend phoned to say they were leaving the country and would the Salvation Army have any use for an interior sprung mattress? Would we indeed!! I was in bed by 8.p.m. that night, and thanked God for what I still believe to be His personal provision for me. When we later left Burma I gifted it to an old retired Officer. He had it covered in red velvet and gave it pride of place in his house!

We also had a special cupboard in which all the

'English' food from home was kept: tinned mushrooms, chopped ham and baked beans etc. When visitors from home came to visit, they usually brought us something for the cupboard, and then, when either of us was off colour we would choose something from the cupboard as a pick-me-up. Pat Riley, an Irish priest whom we had met on the ship out from Liverpool had been really ill in hospital in Rangoon, and came to stay with us to re-coup. He had lost over two stone in weight and it was felt he needed to 'fatten up' before going up country again to his posting. I showed him our treasure cupboard and allowed him to choose one thing every day – and how he enjoyed it! Railton reminded me that we would probably have nothing left by the time he went – and he was right. However, just four days later, I had a call from the British Embassy to say that a box of second hand clothes were being sent, and would I be there to receive them? The parcel arrived by taxi and when the first layer of clothes was removed there were the replicas of all the food we had shared with Pat Riley – tinned salmon, tinned mushrooms, and even baked beans. It taught us both a big lesson, and over the years we have always found that we receive far more than we give.

When we returned to England in 1966, the Army were obviously aware we had had a difficult time the last few months, if not years, in Burma. The pro-Communist regime (with General Ne Win as Prime Minister) had instigated many 'clampdowns' in the country, and we were aware of being observed wherever we went. There was a military car parked outside of the compound gates for four months before we left and it was not a good feeling. One month before we left a large military vehicle arrived at the front door loaded with balustrades and barbed wire. A fence was then erected around the school buildings and maternity unit – leaving access to only the boys' home. We were informed that there would be a new headmaster and fresh teachers and that the existing staff would be told to leave immediately. This caused a great deal of anxiety for all concerned and Railton phoned THQ for guidance. The result was that the Australian Officer then in charge of the command stated that he was sure the best thing was for him to stay in Rangoon, as he knew Railton could handle the situation! We felt very let down by the whole thing. It is amazing how small children can be aware of upset and intrigue. We never knew quite how our feelings were known to Christopher, but the next time we visited Rangoon THQ, Christopher first of all kicked the Brigadier hard on the shins, and then, when the Brigadier picked him up, and said: 'Oh come on now, let us be friends', Christopher got hold of his nose, held it in a firm grip, and twisted it round. It was obviously sore for a couple of hours afterwards and I thought: 'Well done my son.'

We had made several good Burmese and Embassy friends during our time in Rangoon, and during the last few months we received hand written courier letters from them, saying they, too, were being watched, and felt it better that we did not see each other again. All very sad. The government allowed us ten days to leave. We were not allowed to take any personal goods but were allowed one change of clothing for ourselves, and three changes of clothing for the children. No crockery, cutlery, ornaments fabrics – all of which we had taken into the country upon entry. We then had £400.00 in the bank, but were allowed only £100.00. All other goods we gave away to Officers and friends – a wind-up gramophone and records were especially hard to part with as we had no wireless. There were problems in getting Christopher's exit visa, because (having been born in Burma) he was not on our passports! They said: 'You cannot leave with more children than you arrived with.' We had to get official notification from the British Embassy before we had his exit visas and these were worrying days for us.

We were of course not the only ones to be sent out of Burma at this time. Indra was a member of the very large South Indian community in Rangoon at the time, and she offered her services to us as a cook and ayah. She did an excellent job. Her cooking was limited but tasty, and her care of both Janet and Christopher was grounded and careful. Our family was completely adopted by hers and

we enjoyed many Tamilian meals during birthdays and other special times with them. I often look back to these early years for us as a new and young family in trying times, and am grateful to Indra and her own young family (pictured here with us one last time before we left Rangoon) for her help. At the same time as we were told to leave, Indra's family were given the choice of taking on Burmese nationality, or 'returning' to India. They decided to go to Madras and were able to settle there.

Another of the Indian 'exiles' from Burma who was close to us, was Inbam. She was one of the girls in the Girls' Home, and both exceptionally bright and a keen member of the timbrels group (she is playing here just on my right). Originally from a Tamil family, Inbam also moved to India at this time, and worked for the Salvation Army for a while in Madras, before entering the Telegu-speaking Training College for Officers. Despite having to work in several languages at the same time, Inbam

came top of her session, was sent for extra training in Australia, and became a very fine single Officer. When we left India in 1975, we left her enough money for a dowry, and a couple of years later she wrote to us, requesting that she be allowed to buy herself a motorcycle with the money instead! Having served in a number of different roles, she eventually became Chief Secretary of the India Central territory.

We flew from Rangoon to Bombay, and then embarked on a P & O Liner from Australia to England. On the ship, Janet and Christopher had custard for the first time – and loved it! I also gave Janet (then five years old) chocolate for the first time. 'What do you do with it?' she asked. An important happening for us on the ship was that Major (Dr) McAllister, who had been at Dhariwal hospital for many years, was most encouraging of Janet's progress. She had been born with what is known as 'a side-face presentation', and high forceps had been needed to help her into the world. The bruises of the forceps were on her forehead and behind her ear, and as a new-born she looked decidedly battered. When we left England the full extent of her injuries was not known, but later a Doctor in the Seventh Day Adventist Hospital where Christopher was born told me that Burma was an excellent place for her to be. About every three weeks, she used to have a seizure, and I would just lay her on the floor and allow her bare, unrestricted body to thrash about until it finished. Every night we massaged her arms and legs, and noticed that her left leg was not as strong as the right. As soon as she was able we brought a little tricycle – strapped her left foot to the pedal and she would need to push hard so that the wheels turned. It is true that the good leg did most of the work but the left leg just followed suit. Swimming was also a very important part of her recovery and we went swimming every Friday afternoon. She limped a little out of the pool but once in the water she swam like a fish, and kicked both legs well! Dr. McAllister was obviously interested in her case, and during our time on the ship, he conducted several 'fun' tests of strength and agility with her. He afterwards told us that he had never seen such an improved case, and made a report to the South Asia Department to say this.

Looking back, I realize that our work in Burma was very much worthwhile. The work was very small and there were only nine missionary officers and seven National Officers. I remember being very hot, very tired, and very pregnant one day and saying to Railton: 'Are you sure we should be here? It seems a long slog for me, and I am not sure how much more my body can take of this heat.' Railton reminded me that: 'We are building for the future. One day some of these boys and girls will be officers, and Burma will be a Territory and the work wide-spread.' And how right he was! There are now 2,500 soldiers and over 125 Officers. I feel that that those were our best years, as far as youth and enthusiasm were concerned, and they were spent in the right place, with the God-blessed result.

Once we arrived back in England, we stayed with my Mum and Dad in Norbury most of the time, and also visited Railton's parents in Winchester. I always felt on edge in Winchester, and was very aware of the fact that

Audrey (Railton's sister) and her three children lived in the basement with very little communication with us. I felt it to be a strange set-up, but when I asked questions was told: 'it was her choice.' In later years, I grew to understand the situation a little better, and also got to know Audrey well, and to appreciate just how complicated life was for her. She was very fond of Railton, despite the differences in their age and the course their lives had taken. After Railton's death, Audrey and I started to make plans for our joint retirement in the Williams family home in Tavistock; but she also died young, succumbing to cancer in 1989. I often think about the times we might have had together in Tavistock.

On homeland furlough we were expected to do quite a bit of 'specialling' – talking about our time in Burma. One of the requests was for 'Mrs Williams' to speak at the International Training College at Denmark Hill for 20 minutes and the thought of this frightened the life out of me. I pleaded with Railton to say he would speak instead of me but the answer came back, from the College, that 'as it was ladies' day, Mrs Williams is invited to speak, not her husband (though he may attend).' Whilst in Training I had stuttered quite badly and had therefore attended King's College Hospital for speech therapy lessons. It was thought that listening to the bombs when learning to speak had affected my speech, and I received special tuition. Major Fleur Booth was my house officer and knew of this impediment. Now seven years later, I had returned to speak about Burma with only about three stutters. She had been at the Training College meeting and afterwards she marched up to me (she marched everywhere!) and said: 'Many congratulations – it was wonderful.' I said: 'Well, Major, my husband has been a great encouragement to me', trying to give him the credit due. She looked down her large Booth nose and said: 'Your husband? No. It is  the grace of God.' Poor Railton visibly shrunk an inch.

When we were away specialling Janet and Christopher stayed with Mum and Dad and Ann in Norbury. There were language problems because both Janet and Christopher spoke a mixture of Burmese, Tamil, and English – often in the same sentence. Christopher had particular problems with his verbs, and would say things like: 'Grandpa, my legs are nyoundering' – the last word being a version of the verb to hurt in Burmese with -ing on the end. He thought he was speaking good English, but Mum and Dad were perplexed. When we went away again, we left a list of English verbs with their Burmese equivalent, and things improved as far as understanding was concerned. Janet tried to help, but did not really understand why their mixed languages were not understood. I well remember going shopping in order to buy some biscuits. In Burma we had two kinds of biscuits – salt and sweet – and that was it. No cream or jam or any other sort. I went into the supermarket and was faced with six rows of different kinds and was so flummoxed I came home without having bought any!

Towards the end of our time on furlough in England we had an interview with the then Secretary for Asia. We had already stated that we were willing to go back to the mission- field, but knew it could not – sadly – be Burma. Our interview was somewhat bizarre in that the Commissioner thought our new appointment was to Korea. He waxed lyrical about the boys' home there, and was sure we would be happy. He also asked if we were planning to have children (though this must have been in his notes). His assistant just sat and smiled and nodded, not blinking an eye-lid to anything that was said in the interview. The Commissioner then suggested we should pray together, and for five minutes asked that God would bless us in our new venture. I opened my eyes and looked at his assistant when the word 'Korea' was mentioned again, raising my eyebrows quizzically. His re-action was to shake his head, silently say 'No', and close his eyes again. We were then ushered out of the presence of the Commissioner and assured that our next appointment was to a hospital in India!

CHAPTER THREE

PASSAGE TO INDIA

1966-82

'Surrenden', Cooonor, Tamil Nadu, South India.

Ahmednagar and Surrenden: 1966-69

Our first appointment in India was to work at the Evangeline Booth Hospital in Ahmednagar, Maharashtra. We were met at Bombay by Major Gordon Bevan and taken to stay the night at the Red Shield House near the Gateway to India and the back-to-front Taj Mahal Hotel. There we met an Australian couple (whose name I have forgotten) who had two children and had come to serve up country. They had arrived two days before us but were so horrified by the conditions around them that they were both in a state of shock. The woman's main worry was that they could not get Kellogg's Corn Flakes as they always had cornflakes for their breakfast! She also wanted to know where the nearest Salvation Army thrift shop was, as she had seen lots of children without shoes and she was sure her home corps would be willing pay for these shoes for the children. Suffice to say that they had been given no guidance as to what life might be in India and they were sent home on the next ship – never even going to their appointment.

Ahmednagar was (and still is) a Military Garrison town. The journey by train from Bombay was long, hot, and uncomfortable. We noticed the bare and barren countryside around us. The Indian ladies wore their saris tucked between their legs and mostly carried heavy loads on their heads. The men all wore white shirts and dhotis with little black 'Nehru' caps. Railton's appointment was as Hospital Manager. Our home was a sand and clay built bungalow, with a beautiful garden, set in the middle of field of *jowar* (sorghum wheat), and situated about a mile from the hospital. It had a tiled roof, but underneath was a canvas covering pinned to bamboo poles. All sorts of things lived up there and when we painted the roof space we found lots of dead things up there too! It must have been from 'up there' that the snake came one day to visit me. We often saw snakes in the garden, but I did not know they were in the house. I was sitting in an easy chair one day, knitting a cardigan for Janet. Suddenly from around the back of the chair came a cobra. It looked at me from a distance of about 12' at shoulder height, and then spread its hood. I had learned that this was the time it was preparing to strike – so I decided to strike first! I screamed, ripped the needle from my knitting and pushed the half circle of snake away from me. The cleaner came running and said: 'This one you bite – you quickly dead.' I shook and cried for quite a while, but afterwards learned that at that exact time of that day Mum and Dad were praying for me in England.

Ahmednagar was the first place we had a refrigerator and how we enjoyed our cold drinks. *Nimbu pani* was our favourite – boiled water with squeezed lime and sugar syrup; and home-made ice-cream was now possible, too. Janet and Christopher used to take a drink of the lemonade and a jam sandwich and go down the road, by themselves, for a picnic. They thought it was such a long way, but I could always keep them in view and they thought it was very special to go without a grown up. Our water supply came at 5.a.m. every morning and lasted for one hour. Three oil drums were therefore filled and that had to last all day.

The veranda of our house on Pottinger Road was a special place for us as a family, for that is where we had our Sunday lunch of mutton *pilau*-rice, nuts, chopped eggs, and lamb with fried onions. This is one of my special memories of India, for we were all together as a family. I realised that soon not only Janet, who had gone to Hebron, the girls boarding school for missionary children in the Nilgiri Hills very soon after we arrived in India, but also Christopher, pictured here at a birthday party with one of his primary school friends on the front lawn at Pottinger Road, would be away; these treasured times would be no more.

I gave myself about two weeks to unpack and settle down and then asked the Matron what my role was in our new appointment. 'Have babies,' she said – and looking back that was what the preceding three Managers' wives had done. It was really her way of letting me know that I was not wanted on the hospital compound. I decided that if I was not to go to the Hospital, the folk must be invited to me, and I soon had two Bible Classes for anyone who wanted to come in our front room, together with a women's group at which we sewed and knitted garments. After some time, Matron suggested that I could offer English lessons to the nurses. Before coming to the hospital, they had all been required to sign forms confirming that they could read, write and understand English. It was a silly requirement, to be honest, and it was soon discovered that on arrival, many of the trainee nurses answered the question: 'What is your name?' with the same answer they gave to the questions: 'Can you speak English?' and 'Where is your home?', namely: 'Yes, Madam.' The classes were hard work, but fulfilling. In one class we were working on homophones, and I asked them to explain the difference between 'palm' and 'bomb.' One of the girls, who hardly ever spoke, raised her hand, stood up, pointed at her palm, and said: 'This is palm. Bomb is war-like device of explosive nature.' She then sat back down, clearly very pleased. In another one of the classes, we were doing opposites. Having discussed different examples of things that were narrow, I asked for an example using the word 'wide'. Several hands shot up, and the girl I chose proudly explained: 'Mrs Williams is wide.'

Early in 1967 we had the visit of General Fredrick Coutts. He had been our Training Principal so Railton and I were not only thrilled to have him visit us, but very pleased to see him again. Several Retired Officers asked permission to see him, but the Territorial Commander decided that was not to be allowed. They were very disappointed and obviously annoyed at this decision. The result was that when we took our distinguished visitor around the general men's ward in the hospital, six of the retired officers – all in their red tunics – rose as one from under the white sheets of the bed and saluted the General. They had been able to convince the Doctors that they were all sick enough to be given a bed in the ward!

Later that same day, the evening meeting was held, and I was to play the organ for the service. As I walked down the three steps to the organ my ankle gave way and snapped on a big stone. Several people said they heard the sound, and I certainly felt it! A helpful man looked at my foot, which was at right angles from my leg, twisted my foot round and said: 'Now it's in the right position.' I was in a great deal of pain but managed to pump the pedals and play for the important service. When I looked down my ankle was the size of a foot-ball, and I realized something was wrong. I was operated that same night and put in a high plaster. Railton came into the operating theatre to see the Doctor frantically poking down inside the the plaster cast, and saying: 'We've made a dreadful mistake Captain – we've lost your wife's toe. We must have bent it backwards.' Railton was able to inform a very relieved crew that I had no little toe on that foot, having lost it in an accident as a child! About three weeks after I had had the plaster on, I asked the Doctor to please remove it, as I felt 'something' was down there. He was very loath to act, and said patients often had itchy feelings with these plaster of Paris casts. After another few days, he agreed to make a window where I felt the scratching, and three live cockroaches walked out. I felt more than justified in my complaint.

In May of 1967 I was thrilled to know that another baby was on the way. Christopher would be going to school in September, and the new baby would arrive in August. I felt the timing was good except, for the fact that I would be heaviest all through the hot weather. Soon after the visit of General Coutts all the missionary staff decided that we would have a picnic at a place called 'Happy Valley' – about an hour's drive from Ahmednagar. We were in the middle of our picnic by Pimpalgaon lake, and saw that further down the valley some small boys were throwing stones at a tree, but we took no notice. Suddenly the air was filled with a black cloud and a loud humming noise, and it was making straight for us! There really was no escape and we were quickly all involved in this dreadful happening. Railton lost his glasses – without which he was almost blind. Melvin (Dr) Briesman seemed to be almost distraught with pain in his eyes, and both Joan Briesman and I were just trying to run from the swarm, and perhaps dive under the water in the lake to escape: Joan with her daughter Joey, and I with Christopher. Thankfully the children had stings only on their foreheads, and it was afterwards estimated that the swarm had been at a height of three foot and upwards. Although we had a vehicle, Railton could not see to drive and Melvin was crying in pain, so Joan Briesman drove to Meher Baba's house, nearby – where, fortunately, Dr William Donkin, an eccentric but brilliant English Doctor who was a follower of this 'Holy Man', and kept a red Bentley which he called The Blood Clot, was able to treat us as best he could. Just two years later, as Meher Baba lay dying, Melvin was called on to assist and bring oxygen from Ahmednagar; but neither he, nor Dr Donkin, nor the others present, could save him.

I do not remember being transferred from there to the hospital in Ahmednagar, and I was unconscious for four days. When I came round, I remember hearing a visitor saying: 'I've never seen anybody as badly stung as that. I doubt she will survive!' I could not speak, see or even drink because of the intense swelling, and it was estimated that I had over a hundred hornets in my hair. Railton had a live hornet in his ear – that must have been such agony and torment for him, and the side of his head was swollen for weeks afterwards. My greatest sorrow was that I lost the baby I was then carrying (at six months). He was a little boy. It was about two months until I felt anything like normal again. For the first two weeks, I had huge wheals all over my body (as had Railton), but worse still was the loss of the baby. I felt cheated and denied. The Psalms of David became very important to me at this time. He had not known the exact conditions which I was experiencing, but he had known times of deep disappointment, and his words appealed to and comforted me.

Every year during the hottest months of the year, all the missionaries would travel from their appointments up to the hills in order to share their holidays with their children. The large, sprawling house where we stayed was called 'Surrenden', and was very special to us. During the long hot months of hard work and physical toil, we would think of the time when we would, once again be with our children, and this promise would keep us going. The two schools where our children studied were Hebron (for girls) and Lushington (for boys): the former at Coonoor, and the latter twelve miles or so up the hill at Ootacamund. They were good schools and the standard of teaching was generally of a high standard; but there is no doubt that some of the teachers were strange to say the least! The lady in charge of the youngest girls had deaf aids in both ears and, when the youngsters first left home and came to the school, and there was quite a lot of resultant crying at night, she would just remove the deaf aids so as not to be affected by the crying! One of the punishments in the little boys' dormitory was to remove one of the wooden slats at the base of the bed (under the mattress) meaning that, at one time Christopher had only two slats out of the usual seven on his bed: rather uncomfortable and unsafe for a little boy of eight years old! Some of the teachers had come to India hoping to be of service on the plains in various mission stations, but because of incompatibility or ill heath had then decided to teach at the schools. This meant that people who were able to be on the plains were either idealized and held up to the children as 'perfect parents', or else looked upon as people who should have had their children with them and not sent them away to boarding school to be looked after by other people!! How we, as parents would love to have had our children with us, but it was not practical or allowed by the Salvation Army. We were expected to send our children away and just 'pray them through' the years of separation. I remember feeling physically ill every time the train went out of the station, and not being able to operate properly for at least the first week of their being away.

Our holidays were therefore very special times. First of all, there would be the journey from our various appointments to Coonoor. For some of us it would take three days and four nights, and it was a dreaded long, hot, and dusty journey. An order for a large block of ice would be made, and this would be delivered just before the train started. It would be housed in a huge tin bath, and during the journey the ice would melt and we would benefit at least for the first day and night from the cool air. Of course, air-conditioned carriages were not known then (or at very least not available to missionaries). During the journey, other missionaries who worked at various places we visited would join us on our journey, just as, by the time we got down into Madras, the chants of *'chai, chai, garam chai'* from tea vendors would change to *'carpee, carpee, carpee...'*. Then at Madras we would all get off the train, along with our many cases and head for the nearest eating place for *masala dosai*. We were pleased to see each other after one year at our appointments, and had so much to share; and our thoughts were all on seeing our children within the next few hours. From Madras we would go to Coimbatore, then still a fairly small town on the plains, before changing trains again to Mettupalyam. Here we would get on the hill train, the Blue Mountain Express, up to Coonoor. We would so look forward to seeing first the dense forest and later the high hills of the Nilgiris, and later feeling the cool breezes around us as we climbed ever higher.

There were several different buildings in Surrenden, and on arrival we would be shown to our allocated room. The first year we went I remember feeling very 'second class', as Mrs Major Rhoda Griffiths opened the door of a very small room in the 'annexe', in which there was a double bed and two small bunk beds, saying: 'It is small but, of course, you've only got two children.' At the first

meal we learned that the 'normal' missionary family consisted of four, five and six children – we were way behind!

We soon grew to love 'the annexe', its small veranda, and the gardens around it. Breakfast was brought to our room by the bearers. On the tray was papaya, bananas, boiled eggs, toast butter and jam, together with a large pot of tea. We felt pampered and cosseted and really enjoyed these times together. The evening meal saw adults and children served separately, with adults round the table in the large dining room of the main house, but afternoon tea was something very special. Every family would be served with their own tray, on which there would be scones, with butter and jam, specially home-made biscuits, tray bakes and small cakes (or good slices of larger cakes), and, again, lashings of tea. Because lunch was not provided at Surrenden we were really hungry by tea-time and fell upon the food, all of which had been made in the kitchen that very morning, and tasted so very good! We would sit at various round or square tables on the lovely veranda or on the big lawn in front of the house, and put the world (and particularly the Army world) to rights.

During the holiday the date for the 'Annual Picnic' would be announced, and everyone made sure they were available for that. The bearers would spend the morning preparing great dishes of mutton curry, vegetable curry, and egg curry, together with all the accompanying poppadoms, chutneys, and sambars, and gather together all the cutlery and plates necessary. The shout would then go out that we were starting to go, and the snake of people would wend down the long road to the golf course at the bottom of the hill. Once the picnic was spread out we were free to help ourselves to the many dishes available, and eat to our heart's content. The children would eat a little, play a lot on the grass or in the stream, and then return for more food, and usually all that had been provided was eaten by us all. How we enjoyed these gatherings and how special we felt to be part of a group of like-minded folk and to be with our children.

While on holiday that first year, I felt I should start some sort of physiotherapy for the TB patients. The hospital had a large ward with 40 women who, apart from taking their medication from day to day had no stimulation, or reason to try to get better. Their families were not keen to visit for fear of getting TB and even the nurses were very loath to go in and give the necessary nursing services. It was a smelly, dark and depressing place. I managed to get Railton to say the ward could be renovated. Instead of the usual whitewash (which quickly became stained) we chose light blue. All the bedsteads were painted royal blue and then, to further shock everybody, the ladies cut out and painted large figures of the sun – which we pasted at intervals rounds the whole ward. We made hills and trees out of sugar sacks and little roses out of bottle tops, the main point being that the ladies were walking around the ward talking to each other. The whole atmosphere of the ward changed. By the November of that year I realized I did not feel well – went for tests and was scared to learn that I had a 'shadow' on the lung that could be the beginning of TB. So many of the nursing staff (missionaries included) said nothing but looked at me as if to say 'I told you so.' This rather shook me but I decided that I had done what I felt I should do at the time.

Looking back, I think I was low after the stings and particularly having lost the baby and therefore more susceptible to the disease. Of course I did not work in the ward again but one of the long term patients continued to do the physiotherapy with them – and I continued to provide sugar sacks and bottle tops! I had then to start on a six months course of medication which at times made me feel quite ill, but at least when it was over the x-rays said all was well. Around this time Melvin Briesman suggested that I start a Bible class at home with the nurses because I would have a chance to share the gospel, and it would help the nurses in their understanding and usage of the English language. It would also get them away from the Hospital compound for a couple of hours, and be an 'outing' for them.

I decided to teach St Mark's Gospel with the help of William Barclay's commentary. This book had come with me from Burma, and now became particularly precious. It was helpfully presented in complete units so that I could study and think how best to present it to the nurses. The study was announced, and at first we had less than a dozen. I put colourful comfortable *dhurries* on the floor – served tea and biscuits, and within a month we had 40 – 45 attending. All were ready to listen, and contribute to the discussion we had together. The studies continued for two years, and I found them to be challenging and fulfilling. Many of the nurses had a definite head knowledge of the parables etc., but I think few had ever thought as to how it should affect their lives.

Bombay and Anand: 1969-71

Our next appointment was back to Bombay, where we had first landed in India: Railton was to be Young People's Secretary for the Territory and I was to run the Red Shield Guest House. This was a surprise for both of us. Railton was definitely not a Young People person and found it difficult to follow Major Dudley Coles and his wife Eva – they had received a great deal of funding from Canada (their home territory), and so had been able to fund so much and so many. For my part, I had never been in charge of a ninety-bedded hostelry before. But these were our orders, and, having prayed about it, we knew we would have to give it our best.

Although I had imagined running the Red Shield

would be just general administration of bedding, meals, and money, it was in fact far, far more. These were the days of Flower Power, and many young people were travelling the world for the first time. The Beatles had visited India and it had become the 'in thing' to visit various Ashrams and spend time with Holy Men. It was a time of great searching for these young people, and many a long night was spent on the veranda talking things through. It would be good to know what happened to some of those young folk, and to know whether they followed their high ambitions and the declarations of peace and justice for all. But they spoke very little of home: they came from Nowhere and went on to Where-ever-it-was, and for most of them I shall never know how things turned out. The charges at the Red Shield were very reasonable, and we were full nearly every night. There were six twelve-bedded dormitories, and a few other rooms with four and two beds. The hot showers were always popular, and it was good to see bedraggled tourists perk up after a shower and a good meal. For breakfast they had eggs cooked to order and as much toast as needed. The Germans often ate nine slices in one sitting! At night we would do hearty Western-style meals like Fish and Chips, meat pie and vegetables, and Spaghetti bolognaise – followed by apple crumble, jam tart and bread pudding, all with lashings of custard. They loved it all! I always felt the Army did a good service here. The folk were a long way from wherever home had been and the Army filled this gap for a few days.

Whether they had travelled from Australia or Europe most of these young folk had been on the road for many weeks or months and were run down and even ill. This was long before the age of fast jets and package holidays, and most had travelled over land and sea and needed the comfort food we offered. Many would book in for two days and stay two weeks. Most paid their bills regularly and willingly but some not so. A few felt it their right to 'get help' from the Salvation Army. This annoyed me, because I knew that all the money we made went to run the Salvation Army Jubilee children's home in Bombay, and they needed the money to keep going and develop. I knew that many of the young folk received money from home, but that the Post Office and Bank services were not always reliable, so they were allowed to be a week overdue but no more. Most of them knew this, and would borrow off each other if necessary. One day a huge Australian chap had not paid for three weeks, despite several requests, and I decided we must do something. I put all his things in black bags, placed them at the entrance, and locked his room. He was livid and, having seen his things at the entrance of the Red Shield, came roaring up the stairs to the office. There were two flights up to the office, and so I heard the noise and quickly came to the top of the stairs. He was in such a temper that it was obvious to everyone who saw him that he would have hit anyone in his way – even me, a woman. From self-defence (I promise), I put my foot out, caught him off balance and he went spinning down the stairs. The staff then pounced on him and bundled him and the rest of his stuff out of the entrance. The next day eight people paid out-standing bills! Railton was up country at the time, and afterwards I did feel ashamed of my action, but at the time really thought it was a case of him or me. Certainly lessons were learned from the experience.

One day when were very full the doorman, a huge South Indian man who went by the name of Dum Dum, came up to the office and said that a recently arrived English couple had specifically asked to see me. They were John and Ann Wallwork, who later became special friends. They had driven their Land Rover from England, had problems in Kerala, with the vehicle, and decided to see the rest of India by 3rd class rail. When they arrived at Bombay, they had been four days on a train (which had had all sorts of stops and starts because of rioting), and were both dehydrated and ill, Ann particularly so. When I saw them I felt I must help. Railton was up country auditing so I put them in our spacious bedroom, with its own bathroom and a huge ceiling fan. I slept on the veranda outside our dining room. After four days a double room in the Red Shield became available, and they stayed for three weeks. During this time (which I believe was a complete convalescence for them), Railton returned from the audit, and together the four of us put India, England, and the whole world to rights in our long conversations. Janet and Christopher also came home for a few weeks at this time, and Ann thought Janet was wonderful. They had no children of their own but Ann declared that if children 'were delivered at the same age and the same lovely character as Janet, she would order two.' John and Ann went further on their trip around the world and from Singapore came a lovely parcel of ribbons and hairclips for Janet. When we returned from

India in 1971, they allowed us to stay in their lovely pent-house apartment in their marvellous manor house at Wiggenhall-St-Germans. I was also grateful that after Railton's death I was able to spend many week-ends with them in Norfolk. I then was working at IHQ and found life in general boring and difficult. To be able to look forward to going and staying with them and not to think or talk 'Army' for a day or two was a true blessing for me. They both made me feel special and important to them and I was, and still am, grateful. I firmly believe that at certain times in my life God has placed particular people to help me and John and Ann were certainly two of these.

We were not happy to be appointed to the Emery Hospital in Anand; we did not particularly want to return to hospital compound life, as we were enjoying our time in Bombay and felt we were doing good work. Major and Mrs Bennett had been at Anand several years and were well loved in the area. Arnold was a fine fund raiser, and could charm money out of anyone, but he had been taken unwell, and the hospital needed a substitute manager. Jean was known as, amongst many other fine things, a frenetic housekeeper: I once memorably enjoyed a coffee in her house only to find a tea bag in the bottom of the cup! The quarters formed part of the Emery Hospital compound, a large piece of land near the centre of the town. It had been given to the Army for specific use as a hospital and so was purpose built. We soon found that Gujarat was far more prosperous and forward looking than Maharashtra. The huge Amul diary was down the road, making butter, cheese and milk powder. The pasture around Anand was lush and the buffaloes and cows looked like elephants in comparison to the skinny cows in Ahmednagar we were used to.

I soon learned, however, that I was not part of the staff – I was the manager's wife and as such was not expected to be at the hospital at all. I felt very excluded. The Matron and her brother ran the place like clock-work (and had done so for about thirty years), and there was no place for a person with no nursing qualifications. Railton and I therefore concentrated on village work and most Sundays we would be specialling. The main Corps at Anand was a good sized one. They had a Band and a good Songster Brigade along with a congregation of 50 – 60 folk every Sunday. There were weekly practises and Bible Studies. The Army was very well known and respected in the area, and once we had made up our minds to settle there we actually enjoyed our stay. We were also invited to visit the villages for Sunday meetings and enjoyed this privilege. It was at one of these remote villages that we had a particularly special meal. Railton and I travelled this particular day to a very poor area known as 'the Rann of Kutch'. The Army had opened a hall recently and there were new people attending. There were also nine babies to dedicate! (I used to knit woollen bootees for the babies I dedicated and it soon got around) After the well-attended meeting we were offered chicken curry, which we both enjoyed. Knowing it was a poor area, we took only a small portion of chicken – we knew that the officers and the family would only eat after we had taken what we wanted – and Railton said: 'Thank you very much for the lovely curry we really enjoyed it; and thank you for killing one of your precious chickens.

We really do appreciate it.' Back came the answer: 'Please don't worry. Chicken was sick already.' We both decided that we did not feel so well after that bit of information.

Our house was an old colonial building, across the road from the hospital. This compound also housed the Training College for Gujarati Cadets where Major and Mrs Dudley and Eva Coles (whom we had followed in Bombay) were now Training Principles. We had a small swimming pool in our garden and used it nearly every

evening. During the day when we were busy the monkeys would play in and around the pool – so much so that when Janet and Christopher came home on holiday, they were loath to share, and tried to frighten the children away. Over the pool hung the branches of a large mango tree, which produced luscious alphonso fruit in season. Just as they were coming to fruition (and we were imagining eating the lovely fruit) and old father monkey would take his place at the top of the tree, and within two or three days he would be calling the rest of his family to come and share the fruit. One day after a particularly devastating raid by about twenty monkeys I decided to get rid of 'the old man'. I threw stones at him – mainly missing, but also hitting him several times. At first he looked surprised, but then decided to sit it out. When I got near to him in my throwing, he would just move an arm or a leg and keep on feeding. Finally, I got a good hit on his back-side, and he grunted and visibly winced. He was just finishing a mango and decided to stop me in my tracks. With perfect aim and only one mango stone he dropped it on my head. It bled badly, and I had to have eight stitches in the wound. So much for getting rid of 'the old man'!

In the summer of 1970 we travelled to Coonoor for our holidays as usual, and because there were so many folk at Surrenden that year, it was our turn to stay with Reverend and Mrs Elliot at Underfell. This was a home for orphaned children and, in order to generate funds for their work the Elliots took in lodgers. Each family had a sort of garden house in the massive grounds of the home, and at meal times we were invited into the main house, where the Elliots lived, for meals. The elder girls in the home prepared, cooked, and served the meals for the guests, and they felt it a great honour to do this. Things usually worked like clock-work, but one day when we were there a girl called Yesuratnam dropped a whole pile of dinner plates. The look of sheer horror on her face was sad to see. Mrs Elliot just said to her husband: 'She'll have to go. It's the second time that has happened.' Over the next few days we learned that Yesuratnam had indeed been sent out of the home, and when we asked where she would go we received the non-committal reply about her 'finding her own level.' Although Underfell was in Tamil Nadu, we were living a long way away in Gujarat. When we found her and I explained all this to Yesuratnam, she still wanted to come home with us, rather than be alone in Coonoor, for she had never been out of the home, and knew no-one. She said she could cook, clean and was even willing to do the washing and ironing. She returned with us to Anand, and she worked hard: we looked after her, bought her clothes, and gave her spending money every week. She was soon singing as she worked, and was a joy to have around the house. Her favourite chorus was: *I sing because I'm happy, I sing because I'm free. / For His eye is on the sparrow and I know He watches me.*

A Canadian lady who was working for the Ford Foundation and visited us from Ahmedabad saw Yesuratnam and said: 'I am looking for someone just like that.' So, knowing there would be a good salary for Yesuratnam, we made arrangements for her to go with the lady and work for her. She had her own room – with air-conditioning – and an interior sprung mattress. 'Do you think she would be happy here?' said our Canadian friend. There was also the promise that as well as the Rs.400 per month she would be given the equivalent of anything she saved during the month. Yesuratnam had rarely had spending money in her hand, and so saved a great deal (more, I think than the friend had thought possible)! When the Ford Foundation called our friend back to her homeland, there was enough money for Yesuratnam to buy three sewing machines, hire a little room where she worked and slept, and sell ladies' blouses and do alterations. When we ourselves left Anand, she bought us a beautiful blue linen tablecloth which had drawn threads around the outside and cross-stitched scenes of elephants and palm trees. This is still a treasured possession of mine, and is spread across the table in Tavistock on extra special occasions.

Homeland furlough, and my return to India, alone: 1971

We travelled home to England on the Lloyd Triestino ship, Victoria, from Bombay to Venice. By now both Janet and Christopher were able to look forward and enjoy all that went on around the ship. There was a good sized swimming pool and deck games for them to take part in and, of course, the restaurant for which we had to get specially dressed up each evening, and all the lovely food: mostly Italian spaghetti and pasta, but we also enjoyed the cakes and ice-creams! At Barcelona we travelled on the high wire across the city and marvelled at the many churches there. We walked up and down the *Ramblas* many times and drank coffee in the lovely squares around the city. On the train from Venice to London, Railton decided to shave off his beard. He had grown it specifically to be William Booth in a drama presentation we did for the centenary celebrations in Burma and had liked it so much he kept it! The fact that he had shaved it off pleased me, and as an offering of encouragement I said: 'You know, it makes you look ten years younger', to which Christopher piped up and said: 'Yes Mummy –

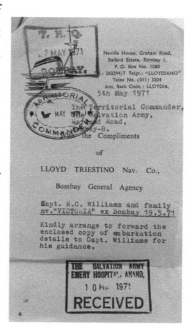

now what are you going to do?' To which I had no answer. As we looked out of the train from Dover to London, we again realised what a 'green and pleasant land' England is, and both the children seemed to be seeing it with new eyes...

We were once again invited to conduct many weekends at various Corps, but there were no language problems for Mum and Dad this time when we left the children with them. Railton's Mum and Dad were now living in Tavistock, so we travelled for a holiday in Devon, and enjoyed the sand and the sea, as well as the cream teas. We had decided that this furlough would not be as busy and rushed as the last, and managed to keep to that plan. It meant we refused quite a few invitations, but we both felt we needed a good rest, and this we had, more or less. Railton took, and passed the accountancy and auditing examinations for the course he had been doing by correspondence over the past two years, and also attended the Army's International College for Officers, a course for future leaders.

Our new appointment was to Calcutta, and because of the fast developing political situation in the new Bangladesh (formerly East Pakistan), the Army changed our plans late in the day and asked Railton to go back to India by air. It was thought a good idea for the children to go with him, so that they would not lose too much schooling. This meant that I went back to India by sea with all the luggage on my own. Suffice to say that it was a nightmare journey for the first few days. I had the whole family's luggage for the next five years, comprising of nine trunks. The Army had promised me that

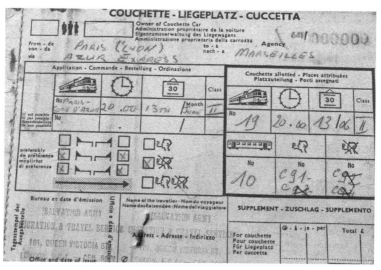

someone would meet and help me from one Paris station to the other. They did not turn up and, in desperation I hired a horse and cart for the transfer. I did not want to have the trunks out of my sight so sat in my Army uniform in the middle of them all, and rode through the streets of Paris, clutching my passport and ticket. I managed to get the second train down to Marseilles by the skin of my teeth, having paid all sorts of people to help me on the way. When I got to my train compartment, I remember sitting on my seat and shaking for at least fifteen minutes. I felt let down and annoyed. At Venice I was met by an Italian Officer who had a large van ready for the trunks. I was so relieved to see him I could have kissed him.

Calcutta: 1972-74

We had never worked in such a dirty, crowded and frenetic city. It was a shock to the system and the THQ was right in the centre of the city. We were in a one bed-roomed flat, half-way up the tall block (which meant the children had to sleep on the veranda when they came home from school), but it was pleasant enough. We found at there was a cross breeze at night, and so left our door open for this. Colonel Fazil Masih was our Territorial Commander and Gordon Bevan our Chief Secretary. Railton was Financial Secretary. The Northern Territory was then a huge Territory taking in West Bengal, the Punjab, Orissa and Bihar as well as Mizoram (which later became the India Eastern Territory). This meant that Railton was very often touring and conducting audits at various Divisional Headquarters and Institutions.

I was asked to be in charge of the Women's hostel

which was part of the same building as the THQ in Dharmatala Street. It housed 45 young women who were career women, when most of their generation were expected to go into an arranged marriage. They had to be strong personalities to even think about leaving home and going to the big city, but to actually do it was admirable. They were nurses from Kerala and the South of India, student doctors from Mauritius and the Andaman Islands, and travel agents from Bengal and Orissa. The rules were very strict for acceptance and entry into the hostel, and there was always a long waiting list. The rates were paid monthly and included breakfast and an evening meal, cooked by the excellent Khansama, whose name was Rhamat. He was quite special and became almost part of our family. He cooked very well for the girls, and was also something of a Father figure to them all. For us he cooked 'esteak' with onions and 'affle pie' with custard, and they were both wonderful! When THQ had Officers councils he would delight in being asked to cook Fish and Chips. I would make sure that he had extra helpers that day and he was in his element – shouting orders and pointing in all directions, but being very much in charge and producing food of an excellent standard.

Of all the girls at the hostel, **Sushila** played the part of the 'poor little rich girl' and really was not mature enough to leave home. She came with her mother and father in tow having come (by car) from a seaside town in Orissa. First of all, her mother demanded a single room – knowing that we had no single rooms. She then said they would pay the double amount, but the other bed in the only available room had already been allocated. After a lot of moaning and groaning, the parents finally bought her things in from the car, in spite of my suggestion that the Salvation Army might not be the place for her. She was in the same room as a lovely Tibetan lady called **Dorma**. Shushila did her best to make Dorma feel so uncomfortable she would leave. One day I said to Sushila (in front of Dorma): 'One of these days I might well ask one of you two girls to leave – and it won't be Dorma.' Sushila looked at me and said: 'Really?' It seemed to settle her down for a while at least. A few months later, the rumour was that Sushila was threatening suicide. She had not done well at college and failed her exam. This was not the first time she had threatened this, and every time it happened the girls would make a fuss of her: buy her sweets and tell her how wonderful she was. I decided enough was enough, and called her into my office for an interview. She was completely unreasonable, said I didn't understand the situation, and that this time she definitely would commit suicide, and that there would be trouble for me if she did. I then said: 'Well in order to help you in this, I will take the other girls on an evening picnic to the Botanical gardens. We will leave around 5.30.pm, you and can plan your suicide, and we will return about 9.p.m. I'll just go through all the details about getting in touch with your parents, so that I can inform them afterwards.' Of course I was bluffing and of course she didn't commit suicide. But I knew it was a high-risk strategy, and made sure I was first up the stairs when we got home from the picnic. Dear Rhamat (who was aware of the situation) had

cooked her a special fish curry with all the trimmings, and she was sitting in the dining room having decided 'it was not a good thing to do.' She never again mentioned suicide, and later married a military officer in a very resplendent marriage.

Connie White was a very studious girl from an Anglo-Indian family from Goa. She was always neat and clean and extremely well dressed – either in a lovely sari or a tailored suit and blouse. Having passed her secretarial training, she asked Railton if there were any jobs available at THQ. At that time Captain Mohan Masih (later to become Commissioner) was having to spend a lot of time away from the office looking after his wife and children. They had been in a most horrific train accident on the way to Bareilly. Mrs Mohan had eighteen main bones broken, and was not, at first, expected to live. She had been thrown from the ladies' carriage, and had been found wrapped around the funnel of the engine. As well as broken bones, she had severe burns. The children were not only injured, but severely traumatised by the whole event. Because Captain was only able to work a few hours a day, Railton employed Connie to work with him. She did very well and was a real credit to his training. She later applied for and got a job in England at Barclays Bank, thanks in part to her CV saying that she had been 'former private secretary to Major Railton Williams of the Salvation Army in Calcutta.'

One day the door man came up to say a young lady had asked to see me in my office. We were full at the hostel and I was ready with: 'Sorry we have no room', but **Parveen** was different. She swept into my office with beauty, grace, and expensive perfume! Her sari was of Benares silk, her jewellery gold, and her bags pure leather. My first thought was that she was a business woman looking for trade, but I was wrong. She explained that she had run away from an abusive marriage, and seen in the phone book: 'Where there's need there's the Salvation Army.' So she had come to us. She had married a Hindu, against her parent's wishes, for she came from a Muslim family. When after two years' marriage she had no children, he began to beat her, tell her she was useless, and suggested she should leave. Her family had, she said, disowned her upon her marriage, so she could not return there. Her plan was to get training as an Air Hostess and thus become independent. I allowed her to stay in the tourist dormitory until a hostel bed became available. Probably because of the unusual entry into the hostel and the change from one room to another Parveen's details were never recorded – a mistake on my part, and probably a relief on hers. Just four months into her stay one of the girls rushed into the office and said that Parveen had collapsed. She died the same evening in the Calcutta General Hospital. Death was due to a brain haemorrhage thought to have been caused by severe blows to the head some time back in her past. I left her body at the hospital and on the way home worried about the lack of details I had: how was I going to contact the family to let them know about their girl?

I need not have worried, for when I got back to the hostel there were two Bentley cars at the front gate, turbaned servants up the stairs, and a very distraught, wailing mother in my office. I then learned that Parveen was a Princess – daughter of Prince Anjum Quder, and a descendant of the last King of Oudh. The family had, it seems, known all along where she was, and had left her alone to 'teach her a lesson', intending to take her back later. The remorse of the mother, Yasmin, was sad to see. She asked all the other girls if Parveen had ever talked to them about her family – no, she had not. She asked if she

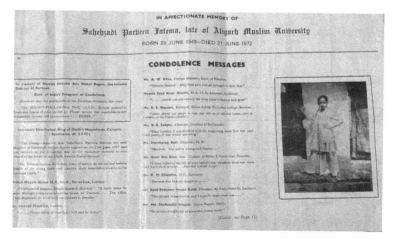

IN AFFECTIONATE MEMORY OF

Sahebzadi Parveen Fatema, late of Aligarh Muslim University

BORN 23 JUNE 1949—DIED 21 JUNE 1972

CONDOLENCE MESSAGES

had been happy at the hostel – yes she had. She put all Parveen's saris and blouses and jewellery in tissue paper and special boxes, and asked if she could buy the Salvation Army bed-spread Parveen had used. I later learned that she had herself come from a Christian family before converting to Islam. Parveen's funeral was one of the largest I have ever seen, and special clerics were flown from Saudi Arabia to conduct the ceremony. Afterwards, her mother gave me a copy of the lavish funeral programme, with messages of condolence from around the world, giving a glimpse of who her daughter had been before she came to us. How humbled I was to be part of the fulfilment of Parveen's expectation of her need, and the Army's meeting of it. This was another of the times when in spite of the sadness, I felt chosen to be especially present for Parveen.

Another person from the hostel I will always remember is **Daulat** the sweeper. He was the only son in a family of nine, leaving him to be responsible for eight of his sisters, before he could be married. Both his father and mother were from the sweeper caste, and very little money was available – none for the education of any of them. Daulat had come at the age of sixteen to work at THQ. He worked from 7 a.m. (mostly on bended knee), doing jobs no-one else would do like unblocking drains and clearing food waste, as well as cleaning and general 'sweeper duties.' Often he would still be in the building at 9.p.m., for the girls in the hostel would send him on errands to the bazaar, often for very little in return. He knew that until the youngest sister was married, he could not think of marrying himself. His sole purpose in life was to save money, so that one by one he could pay the dowries for his sisters. What a drudge his life was, and how difficult it must have been for him! I decided to become his 'agent' in that if the girls wanted him to get anything for them, they would tell me, and I would suggest a price for him to collect at the time of delivery. Of course some of the girls objected and said I was interfering, but I always felt that Daulat had the last word. If he did a job for a girl that was not through me, the cake or whatever it was would be delivered in his sweeper's clothes. If it was 'on the list' and paid a little more for, it would be delivered with his shoes and socks, and the one short coat he had, together with a lovely smile. In time all the girls were wanting the special delivery, putting the requests through me. Daulat thought it was an excellent idea and I always felt he grew an inch or two!

Just as I often think of the young people I knew in the Red Shield at Bombay, so I think of the girls I knew for longer periods at the Women's Hostel in Calcutta. Again I feel that the Army offered a good service to these girls. They were away from their family circle but came to a ready-made home in Calcutta. I know that at least three of them married military officers, two emigrated to England, and one to Australia; and one of the girls from Mizoram later became personal secretary to the Chief Secretary in the Mizoram Government.

Maita, whose father was Swiss and mother American, was an exception in not being from any part of India; she had come to study Ayurvedic Medicine, which in those days was not well known, understood, or much practised in the western world. She was at the Calcutta University doing a PhD, having already completed earlier studies in Germany. She shared a room with an Anglo-Indian girl, Anna and they got on well. This gave me the idea of making a spare room (which was used for storing flour and oil etc) into a six bedded dormitory specifically for women tourists from abroad. They paid three times the price of the Indian girls for the same services, but were generally more than happy to do this as they enjoyed the experience of living with Indian young people; the girls in the hostel all spoke reasonable English and were able to hold a good conversation; and the extra money raised was put aside for new curtains and paint for the hostel – so everyone was happy!

Railton was given responsibility for the monthly transfers and new book-keeping accounts for the new Bangladesh Territory. It was not easy work, more so because London expected everything to be done yesterday, and in the East things just do not happen in five minutes (or sometimes even five weeks). There were lots of angry letters to and fro and at one time I thought we might well be asked to go home. Railton was so insistent things should be done legally and 'with due consideration', whereas I.H.Q felt he was dragging his feet – how little they knew! The crux of the matter was that some of the key government officials were waiting for a bribe, but Railton just played 'dim', and in time everything came through – with no bribe paid. I.H.Q then sent a letter of congratulations in very over the top language saying how wise he was. The other difficulty Railton had was that Major Eva Den Hartog was in

Bangladesh. She did a marvellous job and was particularly adept at handling the media. She managed to accomplish things which others would have never thought possible. But she was also very demanding as far as equipment, money, and sometimes helicopters were concerned!! She was very impatient, but then again she did get things done. Railton was often caught between her demands on the one hand and I.H.Q restrictions on the other, and it was not a good place to be. When she was frustrated in her needs of equipment, she would suggest Railton see to it, and then report him to I.H.Q if it was not done in two days. I.H.Q. would tell him to tell her to wait until the money came through. The art of delegation!

A substantial amount of money which had originally been designated to the Northern Territory had been ear-marked to help the Bangladesh transition. Railton felt that although this was deemed a temporary measure, the money would not be returned – and it never was. We both felt that money was leaking from the Calcutta Red Shield. A very competent officer and his wife were in charge. The place was popular and well run and full most days, but very little money was being sent to T.H.Q. The whole thing just did not make sense. Given my experience in Bombay, Railton suggested that I run the Red Shield. The officer caused quite a stir but as he was being appointed back to his home division in the Punjab, the other officers in Calcutta could not really understand the fuss. Within two months, there was far more money available for T.H.Q – we had made our point.

The Calcutta Red Shield (which has just been re-opened as – to me – a far less attractive modern complex) had a great deal more character to its building than T.H.Q, in that it was an old Colonial mansion made for a large family. It was situated on Sudder Street, right in the centre of the tourist area of the city, with museums, parks and markets nearby. It had a pleasant courtyard at the entrance leading up an old oak staircase to the reception desk. Many of the rooms were round unexpected corners and through small archways – making it different and interesting. Most of the rooms were double, but, on the large verandas there were dormitories for eight to twelve people. The hostel had seventy-six beds in all. Many of the tourists were on the Kathmandu trail, and we saw some weird sights!! As in Bombay, a good breakfast was served, but no evening meal. There were so many cheap eateries around that it was not thought necessary. One service we gave, which I thought was important was that after breakfast every morning, four tables were set out with ham, egg, tomatoes, and lettuce. The guests then bought rolls at the beginning of the line and filled them up to their own choice. The bread rolls were cooked during breakfast and the smell alone got them queueing. Some of the young people who had arrived in Calcutta had come to work with Mother Teresa, and we had a special dormitory put aside for them. I noticed that the workers always knew who they were and treated them with respect.

Jack and Shirley were Australian folk, and a more unlikely couple I had never seen. She was the size of a tank and had a voice like thunder. He was a small and bald, with skinny arms and legs. They had a double room, but did not book in as man and wife. After a few days she declared: 'I like it here – can we stay another week?' During the week I found out that she made all the travelling arrangements, decided where they would go, and held the purse strings. He carried all the bags and did as he was told and their arrangement worked very well.

Tony was an English boy who arrived looking quite ill and tired. I had not seen him for a couple of days, and when I made enquiries, I found out that he had been to a Doctor and been told he had hepatitis. Fearing he would be put out of the Red Shield, he had said nothing and kept clear of me. As this was not at all fair to other people in the dorm, we moved him into a room on his own, and made sure no-one went in there. He had been given his medication, and apart from helping him bathe and eat well there was nothing more to do – he needed complete rest. He slept for nearly four days. I never did find out where he had been, before he came to us but he was surely exhausted. After a week, he was visibly better and after ten days he flew home. His mother sent a letter of profound thanks, together with a donation for the work.

Heidi, a young German girl who was very beautiful, arrived with a boyfriend. She was in a double room immediately opposite the Fairlawn Hotel. This was a lovely old house where mainly middle aged travellers would stay (and I have enjoyed staying there greatly on all my own recent return trips to Calcutta). One day I had a letter from Violet Smith, the redoubtable owner of the Fairlawn, saying there had been a complaint from one of her customers. A young lady has taken to standing by the window of her room to do her breathing exercises every morning – and she was topless! Would we please do something about this! I found out it was Heidi and mentioned the complaint to her: 'If they do not like the view, let them close their window' was her reasonable response.

Our own living quarters was one large room in the centre of the building. There was also a covered veranda stretching around the corner of the building We used the large room as our bedroom and the veranda cut into sections – one for the children's bedroom, when they were home, and one for the dining area. A monkey would come most mornings when we were having breakfast, put his hand through the hole in the netting covering the veranda, and ask for a banana. One morning we had no bananas, but someone had given us slices of salami, so I put one in his hand. He smelled it and then threw it back at me in disgust. I then remembered that monkeys are vegetarians!

One of my main problems at the Red Shield was that there used to be a lot of pot smoked. The sweet sickly smell would at times be overpowering, and I would have to make yet another announcement in the dining room, and put more notices about the place. I hated it and I loathed being the policeman to young people who knew our standards, wanted a clean cheap bed and good food, and yet took advantage of the situation. I also did not like the fact that some of the men in particular did not wash for days. Clean towels were issued every other day, and hot water was always available, but they seemed content to literally stew in their own juice, and the result was far from pleasant. I found it most difficult to first of all suggest they wash, and then, if they did not, ask them to leave.

Because of the nature of my job at the Red Shield I was not able to join in the Army central corps activities as much as I would have liked. The week-end always seemed the time when people 'moved on' from the Red Shield and there was the resultant booking in and booking out. We did always strive to get to the Sunday Morning Holiness meetings, but as Railton was nearly always away, even this did not work out well. I did make a special effort to work with the young people, though, and we had a competent young people's singing company which I enjoyed leading.

There were real difficulties to the work during this time. Christopher, having been taken very unwell at Surrenden one year, was rushed to Nagercoil hospital, where Harry Williams declared him dead. Happily, this was not so, but he was off school for several months, which made Janet very unsettled. There were the sadly all too common conflicts about property and embezzlement which Railton had to deal with as Financial Secretary, and Calcutta was also going through political turmoil, with the Naxalite movement bringing about significant changes, and Indira Gandhi's Emergency regulations imposed on all. Add lock-ins and frequent demonstrations down Lenin Saranee in front of the T.H.Q building to this mix, and you get some idea of how unsettling it could feel. I well remember one particular 'Quit India' march, where the protesters were demanding that all businesses and organisations with foreign backing should be thrown out, and where the band leading the march were playing 'Will ye no come back again'!

Looking back on these years, I feel that as far as spiritual outreach was concerned this was an important time. Many of the young people who were travelling were searching – reading many books on the occult and different philosophical ideas of life the East. As in Bombay, so here, too, they would spend many hours sitting on the veranda of the Red Shield talking things over. They were quite open to discuss spiritual matters, and would ask why I had 'buried' myself in Calcutta. At times like this I again felt special, and was glad the Army had given me this opportunity of sharing my faith. Throughout all the difficulties, political struggles, and sometimes dangers – both within the Army and in country as a whole – which we faced in Calcutta, we had very good fellowship with the Bevans and the Chianghnuna families in particular – sometimes at the Tollygunge swimming pool, for Wednesday evening film nights, or over seemingly endless cups of tea in the late afternoon.

We knew that in 1975 we were due to go home on furlough and had already told I.H.Q that we would not return. After sixteen years away from our homeland we felt we needed to be together as a family. Christopher was now nearly twelve and Janet was nearly fifteen – important years for their education. It was therefore a surprise to receive our appointment to the India South East Territory. Once more we packed our bags and moved on.

Nagercoil: 1975

Railton's appointment was as Financial Secretary to the Territory based in Nagercoil. Our quarters was within the compound of the Catherine Booth Hospital. We later realized that a lot of his time would be spent in checking the accounts at the hospital. Something was wrong and no one was able to trace the reason. Railton finally found out the cash till was being electronically altered every four days to show less takings – thus giving the 'fiddler' quite a large sum annually! One reason we were pleased to be in Nagercoil was that we were much nearer the children. They were now just eight hours on the bus away instead of three days on the train. Janet had been very affected by the death of Shirley Millar, a young and vibrant New Zealander (she and her husband had followed us to Ahmednagar), followed eighteen months later Walter Lucas. He was a highly efficient Doctor who was already putting MacRobert Hospital (in the Punjab) on the map. He was only thirty-four when he died during a very routine operation – completely unexpectedly. Ten years earlier, soon after we left Ahmednagar, Dr Murray Stanton from New Zealand had died from a liver disease bought on by a rat bite. This meant three Salvation Army missionary deaths in ten years. Being stationed miles away from them for most of the year, it was a difficult time for us all when we said our good-byes to the children. With the knowledge that well-loved parents had died in recent years, there was the unknown question for the children: 'And for us? Shall we see them again?'

All through the years of service in India there have

been tragic incidents for missionaries and their children. It is not just being away from your homeland that is difficult. The heat, the flies, and constant noise together with the insidious constant thought that an ordinary illness could mean death – it is wearing and ever present. At this time also Christopher was having recurring bouts of an inner ear infection he caught while he had been convalescing in Calcutta. He used to cry in pain (and boys of eleven try hard not to cry!), but it was obvious it was a deep seated infection. The Calcutta Doctor had not been helpful. He would poke long tweezers down Christopher's ear and say: 'Well it's still there', as if we should be pleased with the news. Once we moved to Nagercoil, where there was less humidity and pollution, the ear infection cleared up.

Catherine Booth Hospital was one of the last Salvation Army hospitals in India to have missionary staff. In charge was Dr Alloway, with his wife and two children, then there was Dr Herb Rader and his wife Lois (and six children), Major Miriam Ward, Captain Janet Cooper, and an English pharmacist (whose name I'm afraid I can't recall, but it might have been Smith!) and his wife (who was an officer's daughter); we were all based on the same compound. Janet was already interested in nursing and when she came home from Coonoor on holiday, she was invited to spend some time in the Mother and baby unit. She was over the moon. Americans we have always found like to play hard as well as work hard. There were lots of picnics on near-by beaches, lots of visitors from other lands who had come to see the fine work done at the hospital, and we were always asked to join in the various celebrations. The Rader family was patriotic and every morning at 6.a.m we heard the 'Stars and Stripes' sung by six voices, a piano, and a cornet. The American children did not go to boarding school – they were home schooled; that was a difficult pill for me to swallow.

One thing I did enjoy at Nagercoil was the Corps. We had a band, songsters and several other different groups for Bible Studies for the nurses and children. At Easter and Christmas, we practised long and hard to give a good account of the meaning of these times to the local people, and they responded well. Several times we conducted spiritual campaigns with visiting preachers and erected a large *shamiana* tent which would be full to overflowing. Again I felt the Army did a good work here, and the hospital was well known for miles around. It was obvious that missionary staff would soon be replaced by Indian personnel, and that many changes would happen to the structure of command in the hospital as a result. Time has shown this to be true, and CBH hospital in Nagercoil currently represents one of the Salvation Army's success stories in this respect. For there was clear forward planning for the transition away from reliance on missionaries, along with appropriate training given to National Officers and administrators as they took on responsibility for the work. At this time, I would never have imagined that I would, twenty or so years later, be serving as Social Secretary for India, and so be involved in the leadership training of National Officers in the full spectrum of the Army's Social work. On a recent trip to Nagercoil while on holiday with my family in the South,

I was especially happy to be able to see all this hard work and difficult change bearing fruit.

Interlude I. Back to England, 1975-1982

Before leaving India, Railton had been informed that his next appointment would be at IHQ in the International Audit department. He was very chuffed about this, and it had been one of his secret 'hopes' on coming home. I don't think either of us realised how often he would be away and for how long. We had left India specifically to make a family unit, but so often the circle would be broken. One thing we were pleased about was that our house was to be in Croydon – within four miles of Norbury, where my Mum and Dad lived. We therefore said we would attend the Thornton Heath Corps with them. However, two days after we had arrived Sergeant Major Albert Ashmore from the Corps at Croydon visited and said: 'Of course you will be attending the Croydon Corps – I'll pick you all up this Sunday and introduce you to the folk there.' It made sense really as Croydon was within walking distance, and Thornton Heath Corps was a lot further away.

Our new quarters was at 80 Waddon Road: a mid-terraced, three-bedroomed house with a pleasant garden to the rear. It needed a lot of 'tlc' but the Army allowed us new carpets, curtains, and kitchen equipment, and also supplied other furniture. We soon settled and felt that it belonged to us. There is no doubt that both Janet and Christopher had difficulties adjusting to life in England. They both tried to give the feeling of 'business as usual' but it was not the euphoric life we had all envisioned when in India. Railton was away a great deal – often for 6 weeks at a time – and this made life difficult for us all. We were well accepted at Croydon Corps and all joined the various sections. Christopher learned to play the drums and later an instrument in the YP Band. Janet joined the very fine Harmony group.

Railton spent every week-end and all his spare time going round the schools in the area. There were some very good schools and some extremely bad ones. At the one nearest to us there had been two stabbings in the past year, and we were warned about drugs being rife there too. We were able to get Janet into the very fine Old Palace Girls' School situated at the end of our road. After a lot of persuasion Railton did manage to get Trinity School at Shirley to agree to let Christopher at least take a late entry exam in French, English, and Maths and then to let him join the second year (with the strict proviso that if he was not able to keep up academically he would be asked to leave at the end of term). After the boarding schools of Hebron and Lushington, any schools would have been a challenge, and so they both were. No doubt they will give their own thoughts and feelings of these important years. Suffice to say that they both worked and studied extremely hard and did more than we expected.

Once again I had no specific appointment of my own, so during the second year of our time at Croydon I saw Major Frank Ward the Commanding Officer, and asked what he would do if he had another officer at his disposal. He suggested I take over the leadership of the

Women's Fellowship meeting – a group of about forty to forty-five ladies who met every two weeks on a Monday. I made some very good friends there and was able to persuade Hazel Brown to become my assistant (and later to wear full Army uniform). The other thing Major Ward asked me to do was fit out and run an Army thrift shop for the Corps. It was intended that a community centre should be built at the side of the existing hall, but money was needed for this. Not many second hand shops were around at this time, so it was a bit of an experiment. Of course there were some people in Croydon Corps who were a bit sniffy about being associated with anything second-hand, but when, at the end of the year they saw the amount of money the shop had generated they had second thoughts about it!

Most of the ladies I invited to work at the shop were happy to do so. The premises we had was up for demolition, but the Army was told it would be three years before this happened. It was situated on the main road into Croydon, with a bus stop right outside. This meant that people waiting for a bus looked in the window, came into the shop to buy and lost their bus! There were always two ladies in the shop serving – I was upstairs sorting and pricing together with Ethel and Emily. These were two sisters who had lived in the same house but had not spoken to each other for 14 years. Emily had worked all her life in a laundry pressing sheets with a heavy steam machine. Ethel had spent her life washing and cleaning for other people. Neither had much education but they were both honest and loyal. offered to help at the shop and while Emily was happy to iron the badly creased things Ethel would go through the pockets (and often found money) and look for brooches or hat pins. She once found a cameo brooch which we sold at Sotheby's in London for £635! Her other job was to make tea for the staff – and particularly any folk who asked to speak to me. To me this was the most important thing we did – we made five soldiers with their first connections being at the shop.

On looking back, I feel that these two things I did in the Croydon Corps helped me to integrate with the folk here. I made some special friends and still hold some very happy memories of those days. As a 'spin off' from the shop I held an Antiques and Bric-a-brac sale at the Citadel every three months. These were quite social happenings for the Corps and were well attended by the general public and enjoyed by the Army folk. Each sale would be in aid of a specific section of the Corps – Songster, Band, Y.P. Band and Singing Company etc. The leaders of these sections were responsible for scones, cakes and coffee and I would be responsible for the sale itself. The articles had all been put aside from the thrift shop during the intervening weeks. I had stalls of linen, lace, silver, glass, jewellery, crockery and small furniture. In time several experts in their field would be happy to come the evening before the sale and advise me on my prices. For doing this they would have first choice of the goods. Because of this it was known that our prices were not cheap but fair. Usually we would make £350 - £400 each and the sections would benefit with this injection to their funds. When Railton and I farewelled from Croydon and were appointed to Pakistan as General Secretaries the folk at the Corps gave us quite a send-off. Commissioner Leo Ward insisted that a special 'after meeting' be held and we sang 'Till we meet at Jesu's feet'. At the time I felt this was a bit unnecessary and morbid – not knowing that Railton would never return to England.

One of the ways I found of being useful in Croydon was to give English lessons to local Asian women in the community centre. There was, to my surprise, some resistance to this from members of the corps. I found that the Army in England was not as welcoming to immigrants as it should have been. A strange story will illustrate the point. One of the songsters was concerned that though we had many girls in the singing company, there were not many boys who stayed on beyond the Young People's Band. I knew that some officers' children would soon be returning from the mission-field, and would be coming to Croydon Citadel, so I said, by way of encouragement: 'The Brown boys will be here soon.' My fellow songster

misconstrued what I had said, and pulling a face, replied: 'Oh, brown boys...' with evident distaste. On one of my recent trips to Croydon, however, things looked very different: all the sections of the Corps seemed happy and integrated with people of colour from all over the world worshipping together. My particular joy was to see my songster friend waving the flag during the meeting, proud to be part of the new Salvation Army of the 21st Century.

Janet left the Old Palace School in the July of 1979 and started her Nursing Training at the Great Ormond Street Hospital for Sick Children that same month, which meant that she missed her summer holiday with the family in Cliff House, in Bournemouth. She had obtained excellent results in her A-level examinations and then, after an oral interview, had been offered a place at the important hospital. We were all thrilled to bits as this was exactly what she had been hoping for. However, this was yet another difficult transition for her as she had to 'leave home' yet again. We managed to get a tiny overpriced room for her in the nursing home near the hospital, but it was pokey, uncomfortable and airless, and it was not long before she decided to come home at weekends and travel back up to London by Lambretta. The year before her training we had noticed a lump on the back of her neck and mentioned it to the Doctor. He was rather dismissive and decided it could be a sebaceous cyst but was definitely 'nothing nasty' – how wrong he was! When Janet started at Great Ormond Street she found that the nodule in her neck interfered with the stiff, starched collars student nurses of the day wore, and was very uncomfortable. She was therefore booked for a fifteen-minute procedure to have it removed, but that afternoon, whilst she was still in the surgery, we had an upsetting call from the hospital. The lump was a secondary cancer. The main cancer was in the thyroid and this secondary cancer had grown around her neck. To say that we were worried is an understatement. She was then booked for a far more serious operation with one of the best surgeons in England for the very next week. It was a four-hour operation and when she came round from the operation her small white face and heavily bandaged neck was sad to see. We had been informed that it might be necessary to take away her voice box but we were grateful to hear her talking and responding as normal soon after the operation. Her neck was cut virtually right round and for a long time she was unable to raise her head and just looked at the world in what she called 'her pavement perspective.'

Over the next year Janet was given two more operations together with a new and radical treatment for those with thyroid cancer, called 'radio isotope treatment,' given in the form of a drink. This powerful cancer-killing drug meant that Janet was radio-active and therefore dangerous to be in the company of whilst the drug worked in her body. She lived in an isolation room for one week, and we were only able to communicate by waving through the glass partition of one wall of the room. This must have been frightening and bewildering for her, but through it all she was calm and trusting. She felt called to serve on the mission field and held the firm belief that she would be healed – and she was! Great Ormond Street allowed her to resume her training, and although she was often very tired she did manage to complete the course, being given her certificate by Princess Anne on the day of graduation.

Soon after this the Army questioned us about our willingness to go back to South Asia and we asked for a time to think about it. I felt it was too soon to leave both Janet and Christopher, but our lovely neighbour Pat made it obvious she thought we should go and promised 'a home' in her house for them both. By now Christopher had been offered a scholarship at St John's College, Oxford to study Modern Languages and they were both doing what they wanted to do in the way of study. We were so proud of them both and thanked God every day for His leading in their lives.

I was also concerned about leaving my Mum and Dad. As it was, my dear Mum, who had been in precarious health for many years, died just two days after moving from Sunbury-on-Thames to Tunbridge Wells. She could not get out of her mind the fact that Dad would die first and leave her to be on her own, and she had heard of the Tunbridge Wells Home for Retired Officers. Her idea was that she and Dad would live there together as long as possible, and that when he died, she would then have people and friends around her. Dad was not keen on moving as he loved his garden at Sunbury with its many old rose trees and fine geraniums. He would stop anywhere and everywhere for new horse manure, and often his car would smell rather badly with the stuff (much to Mum's annoyance)! Two days after arranging the 50th anniversary of the Torchbearer's reunion at Sunbury Court, Mum and Dad moved to

Tunbridge Wells, and the next day she died in the hospital there.

Mum had been very ill several times during her life. She had contracted Rheumatic Fever at their first appointment as Officers and this had left her very weak and susceptible to illnesses. Dad had always managed to pull her through by telling her she had 'wind on the kidneys' (when she was seriously ill with internal bleeding), or telling her that the fish she had for dinner had not agreed with her (when she had severe gastro-enteritus). She would always believe what he said, make up her mind it could not be serious, and get better. This time he could not help and she died of a stomach ulcer which burst. To say my Dad was shocked is an understatement. I remember looking at him and feeling as though someone had painted his whole face in white emulsion. He sat down as his legs gave way under him, and then shot up again, and said: 'I must go to her now.' He sat by her bed for the whole of the night, knowing but not accepting that she had gone.

Because this happened so soon after their move, Dad never really settled at Tunbridge Wells. Everyone was very kind, and he did already know several folk who were living there, but it was not at all easy for him. He still had his car so would come to Croydon every week-end to stay with us. The week-end was then from Saturday to Monday but within a few months it became a long week-end – from Thursday to Tuesday. Often Dad would purchase a weekly low priced train ticket and go, with a special offer £5 ticket for old age pensioners, from Croydon Station to places all over England and Wales. I remember him once going all the way to Edinburgh and back in one, very long, day! He loved exploring, and meeting people, and was learning to love life again. One day as we sat at the breakfast table he said: 'How would you feel if I told you I might get married again soon?' I said: 'I would be pleased, Dad. I have always felt it is a compliment to the first partner to get married again. Do you have someone in mind?' This was only eighteen months after Mum had died, and I confess I did feel it was a bit soon, but I also knew that he was still desperately lonely. 'Well,' said Dad: 'I have prayed about it and I think it should be Margit Gauntlett.'

I remembered then that when Mum and Dad had lived on the London Road at Norbury, Mrs Commissioner Gauntlett and her daughter, Margit, had lived next door. Margit had two brothers who were Sidney and Caughey. Sidney, a Doctor Colonel with his wife Jean were serving in Africa, and Caughey and his wife Marjorie were Chief of the Staff. Dad had often done household jobs for Margit and her Mum, such as repairing dripping taps and blocked pipes, and had generally been a good friend to both. He would also give them apples from his trees in the garden, some of which would later be returned as a lovely apple pie by Margit! The fact that she was 19 years younger than Dad did not seem to faze him at all, but I did feel he was punching above his weight. The next thing I knew, though, was that Dad was asking: 'Do you think this tie goes with this shirt?', or 'When you go shopping next time, would you please buy me a shaving perfume called *Brute*?' I knew something was up! The next big decision was where he would take her for their first date. He was now staying with us in Croydon most of the time, and I suggested a lovely Italian Pizzeria in town, or, alternatively, a place well known for its Roast Dinners. Instead he decided he would take her down to Eastbourne (a journey of around an hour and a half) to a well-known Fish and Chip shop! Rather basic, but obviously effective. Margit retired just ten months early and she and Dad were married at Thornton Heath Corps. She had retired then as Dad was seventy-eight, and they wanted to be sure they had some time together. They actually enjoyed fifteen years of useful and active retirement together, first of all with Margit being in charge at the missionaries' flats in Norbury, looking after folk who were coming and going from and to the mission field, and latterly at Bournemouth. There is no doubt Dad lived far longer than he would have done on his own, for Margit looked after him with more than tender loving care, and we as a family are grateful for those extra years.

CHAPTER FOUR

BACK TO THE FUTURE: PAKISTAN & SRI LANKA

1982-93

Lahore: 1982-86

We never know, of course, what the future holds. When we told the Army we were ready to return to the mission field, our appointment was to be Chief Secretaries in Pakistan. We later found out that Gordon Bevan had asked specifically for Railton, and we certainly received a good welcome from everyone in the Territory. There was a busy if not hectic programme of services and seminars going on and within four days of arriving we were 'on tour' and meeting many officers. The Territorial Headquarters was a large three storied building in Lahore, set back from the main road in well maintained gardens. We lived on the third floor and had a good sized main room and kitchen, together with bathroom and bedroom. These were probably the best quarters we had ever had on the mission field during our time away from home.

Pakistan was entirely different from India, considering it had once been part of the same land in days past. We enjoyed a winter when it really was cold and we had to have woollen coats on. We did not enjoy the intense dry heat of the summer, when you felt as if your brains were frying. I was very aware that ladies were considered very much second class citizens, and that the opinion of men only was even considered worth listening to! Colonel and Mrs Gordon Bevan were the Territorial Commanders and we had been friends many years before. Our children often travelled to boarding school together, and Grace and I would cry on each other's shoulders as the children went off to school yet again. Railton was a good 'lieutenant' to Gordon, and they soon struck up quite a formidable partnership. Gordon was excellent at public relations and Railton was good at details and both needed each other. We all travelled the length and breadth of the Territory conducting Officers' meetings and seminars, and trying (and often succeeding) to give our folk ammunition for better service to the community.

Pakistan was known to be a place which generated tension and sometimes open animosity and violence; this had been true for many years, and would prove true in the future. Sadly, this was as true within the Salvation Army as in the country more generally. The tensions were historical, with missionaries having been killed and subject to violent threats in the past, and they would later boil over into the tragic murder of Bo Brekke, whom we met and worked with in Sri Lanka. And yet, as we also found during our years travelling across the territory, there are a great many exceptional soldiers and officers working for the Lord and for the people of Pakistan, all over the country. The Salvation Army World Service Overseas, an organisation I had not even heard of before we went to Pakistan, were an important part of this work: able and keen to fund new projects for many of the out of the way places which had been neglected in past years, and the whole Pakistan Territory benefitted greatly from this interest and funding.

At the time we were there, the Afghan war was in full swing. I remember travelling up to the border of Pakistan and Afghanistan in order to view some land which had just been allocated, by the Pakistani Government, for work with the refugees. The refugees were just beginning to come over the border from Afghanistan in order to shelter from the constant bombing from the Russian troops and the other struggles for power going on. They were mainly wives and children, but some wounded men folk travelled with them to recuperate, before going back into the fray. There was an enormous area which was to be given to the settling of the Afghan people temporarily. The Pakistan government did not want them infiltrating into the main country, and so wanted to contain them in this area. The Army were asked to help. I remember looking over dry, barren land: there was no water, no life of any kind, because it really was a desert area. When Railton and I visited eight months later, the scene was completely different. 24,000 people had come over from Afghanistan, and now were camped on the hillside. It was a busy, crowded place, with streets defining areas of market produce and living quarters, as well as health units, a hospital and a school. Together with this there were several projects where both young and old could learn new skills and hone up on old ones in order to generate funds in future days. Major and Mrs David and Jean Burrows gave excellent administrative and practical help to the project, together with some fine Pakistani and Afghani people we were able to hire to work with the Army.

During this time, with the help of Sue Allibone, an experienced nurse, we were able to start a GOBI programme within the Home League structure of the Territorial set up. This stood for Growth, Oral rehydration, Breastfeeding, Immunisation. The word

GOBI means 'cabbage' or 'cauliflower' in Urdu so the ladies could easily remember this. Sue and I toured the Territory, conducting teaching seminars and meetings on child health matters. Ladies of any religious persuasion were encouraged to attend our seminars and meetings, and it was good to see that the Muslim and Hindu ladies joined in alongside the ladies from the Christian villages. All the women were keen to learn anything new, and although their men folk were a little reluctant, we noticed that they watched from afar, and although we opened and closed in prayer they were happy to go along with our teaching. Most of the people attending were unable to read, so a lot of the teaching was done with pictures and role play and the ladies really enjoyed and benefitted from the classes. The Officers' wives also enjoyed the new importance of learning and then teaching to their people. There was a new feeling of 'doing something very special'

as one of the ladies put it, and they seemed to grow in stature over the months and years. So much so that some of the men Officers were a little concerned at their wives' new found confidence, and reported that many of them were now ready to preach on Sundays!! Some of the ladies soon proved to be better speakers than their husbands. This meant an overall improvement in standards all over the Territory.

Janet and Derek had met on a Christian holiday tour to Austria, just six months before Janet was due to start a two-year stint as a lay worker with the Salvation Army Basic Health Unit in Karachi. They became engaged on the understanding that Janet would fulfil her desire to serve in this way and that Derek would visit within six months. My friend Pat, who had been our neighbour in Croydon, called us specially one day (this was when an international call was a rare thing) to say: 'I suppose you know that Janet has a friend whom she met on holiday – I am phoning you to say I think it is becoming quite serious.' We did know that they were friendly but we didn't know it was serious and Railton did his protective 'Indian father' rant by saying: 'We don't know him and we have never even met him – we can't allow this!' My theory was that if Janet thought he was the one, she was old enough and sensible enough to know and we must give them the benefit of the doubt. Derek therefore came out from England to visit Janet (and us) and we went on holiday together. It was with great trepidation that I met him, and I was actually physically sick just ten minutes before going into the room to see him for the first time. We went up to Coonoor in order that he would see something of the background of her life so far – where she had been to school and where we had holidayed together etc. We all loved the Nilgiri Hills, with Coonoor and Ooty especially, and were really looking forward to 'showing off' India to him. However, the few days we were there, the hill mists came down in no uncertain terms, and although we did our best to explain how beautiful the forests and hills were he could see nothing! He encouraged our enthusiasm and declared that when he visited the next time he would see it all – and he did.

After the India holiday Derek continued to travel around Pakistan whilst we went back to work in Lahore and Janet and to Karachi. During his travels Derek had visited the Christian Technical Training Centre (CTTC) in Gujranwala, a town forty miles north of Lahore. He was encouraged to think about taking up an instructor's post in the carpentry shop, with the promise of accommodation to go with it. This opened up the possibility of Janet and Derek getting married and serving together in Pakistan. The wedding date was set for December 22nd at the Lahore Central Hall. There was great excitement as there had not been a 'European' wedding at the Salvation Army for many years. Mrs Major Mavis Mackerith had offered to arrange the reception, for which I was very grateful. Commissioner John Nelson (The Territorial Commander following Gordon Bevan) had taken it upon his shoulders to do the wedding counselling and part of the ceremony. It had to be only 'part' because there was no Salvation Army representative qualified to do the actual ceremony so a minister from a German Mission was seconded to do this. Derek's Dad and Aunty Rose and my Dad and Christopher had agreed to travel from England. Pauline Hill and Jane Prior had agreed to come to be the bridesmaids, and Derek's friend Jeremy Moody, working at the British High Commission in Islamabad at the time, was to be the best man.

The day before the wedding Janet and Christopher took Dad out for a walk in the famous Shalimar Gardens in Lahore and he fell into a water culvert. This meant that on the day of the wedding he had a large panda eye as he prayed for the couple in the ceremony – meaningfully and well. The main meal of chicken curry was prepared by a team of cooks hired for the day and it was served on the main lawn of Headquarters. There was

a large *shamiana* in which the bride and groom sat whilst people went to congratulate them. We had catered for 250 and invited 250 but in Pakistan the bill is paid by how many plates of food are served and the number was 267. It was then realized that a few folk who were passing probably thought it was a 'free food day' and had taken advantage of the situation! Suffice to say that everyone had ample and the food actually was very good. Because I was worried about my Dad being affected by the rich curry I had arranged to make him an omelette instead of the curry. I raced up the three flights of stairs, cooked the cheese omelette and came downstairs only to find that he was already in the middle of a large plate of curry!! He pushed aside the remaining rice and said: 'Oh, thank you – just put the omelette here – I'm enjoying this curry.'

Mavis Mackerith prepared an excellent evening meal upstairs in the Territorial Commander's quarters, and the young English volunteers who had come from Derek's mission really tucked in to the sausage rolls which Christopher had brought from England. I did feel sorry for Christopher, in that he realized all the sausage rolls had gone (within three minutes of being put on the table) and said to me: 'Never mind, I'll get some profiteroles – I really like them.' When he went for them they too had disappeared. All together it was a lovely day and, of course, in Pakistan you do not have to worry about the weather. We knew it would be a good day and it was!

Two months before our homeland furlough, on one of our trips to the work with the Afghans, I was badly hurt by going over a ploughed field in an open jeep. We were

bouncing up and down and I banged my head hard against the iron ridge of the top of the jeep. I had to be laid flat for the journey home (which was about eight hours) and was in great pain. The result was a six-week constant bed rest on flat boards. I hated it. It was hot, painful and boring and I do not know how I would have coped without Railton's kindness and the visits of friends most afternoons. I had days when I wondered if I would ever be well again, as I had not experienced anything so debilitating before and I found it very difficult. When it was time for us to go home there was a doubt as to whether I would be able to travel, as I had only been sitting upright for four days before we flew. I was doped up to the eye-brows when we flew, so I slept nearly all the way home. But I was certainly pleased to be in England again.

The teardrop of India: 1986-88

During our furlough we were called for a special interview with the Chief of the Staff (Commissioner Gauntlett) and told of our new appointment – to Sri Lanka, as Chief Secretary! We had previously both said that we hoped we would never be stationed there. We had passed through the island on our way to Burma and had not been at all impressed. It was, as General Eva Burrows felt, a 'hot little hell-hole,' and neither of us wanted to go. We were, for all the tensions and difficulties, happy in Pakistan and had quite a few unfinished projects in which we were especially interested. I was particularly frustrated by the fact I had already received funding from American sources for two of these – both for women's projects – but these were not to be. It was a sad situation. and it was with heavy hearts that we left Pakistan.

Our new quarters was outside of Colombo in a place called Bambalapitiya. It was half an hour's ride from THQ, and had always been the Territorial Commanders' house. The new TC's wife had, however, refused to move from her present house in the grounds of THQ in Colombo, so Bambalapitiya became our designated place. We were never very happy there. It was isolated, and we were surrounded by many Muslim households who kept themselves very much to themselves. I tried to invite a few to afternoon tea but had no 'takers', and soon found that the Salvation Army was not known in the area. The soldiers and officers of the Territory gave us a very warm welcome, however, and we were soon visiting different Corps every week-end, getting to know the field and social officers beyond THQ personally. This was Railton's wish: that we knew our officers and, looking back I feel that he went into the accident rather tired and rather low physically after all the travelling. Because we lived so far outside the city, a car was designated to be used by us for travelling – but was rarely 'available'. The TC and his wife and extended family used it very often, but the only time we were allowed to use it was for official visits to the villages. On the day in question, Railton had been told by the TC's wife that he would need to travel into the office by bus, as the car was not available: she wanted to use it herself. I was not travelling with him, so do not know exactly what happened, or why he was in a three-wheeler 'put put' (or 'tuk tuk' as they are also called). He hated them and would rarely go in them, so I can only think the bus was full. Suffice to say that at one of the main roundabouts in the town, an embassy car ploughed right across the 'put put', and Railton was pinned underneath. He lay in the hot sun on the road for two hours before he could be cut out of the result of the crash. By the time I was told about the crash, he was in the general hospital, and when I saw the conditions there I was horrified. The sheets were not clean, the crowd was quite invasive, and the floors around us were stained badly. I felt that I must get him out of there. We therefore transferred to the Nawaloka Hospital, and had private treatment there.

As he responded to initial treatment, I called Janet, and she and Derek came from Pakistan to be with me, and I was so grateful they were there. A couple of days later, Christopher arrived from England, and we were a complete family again. Actually I had thought that the worst was over – how wrong I was. The whole of Railton's left side had been smashed in the accident; his leg was broken in two places; he had four broken ribs, and had lost a lot of blood. He appeared to make a gradual recovery but on 3rd December, three weeks after the accident, whilst receiving physiotherapy, he had a pulmonary embolism and died in intensive care a few hours later. We were all there surrounding him and he seemed to raise his head as though to check we were all there and then just died. We were then told that one of the broken ribs had pierced his lung, causing an embolism, and that was the cause of death. I really do not remember a great deal of what happened that day. I do remember crying uncontrollably and feeling that the end of my world had occurred, but not much else. I know that I was very grateful to have Janet and Christopher and Derek with me, and that Captain Bo Brekke and his wife were especially kind to us all. The TC had to be booked into a nearby private hospital with 'stress' and I did not see him again until the day of the funeral.

Colonel Gordon Bevan (who was on an official tour of India for the Army) was asked by IHQ to conduct the funeral, and Captain Irene Ogilvy (a special family friend) flew from Pakistan to be with us. I will always remember their support and understanding at this time. Officers from all over the Territory attended, and the Colombo Central Hall was heavy with the scent of jasmine wreaths. I do not remember much of the funeral service in the hall or the burial. I just know it was one hot, horrible, and torturous afternoon to get

through and survive. I had always dreaded losing a relative away from England, because of the wailing and cacophony of noise. This was an entirely different sad, shocked, and quiet crowd who gathered, and it was far more dignified than I had expected. The roads through which we passed were full of people, who had come to show their respect for Railton and for the Army. Many of the shops had closed, and hundreds of officers and soldiers followed the coffin on foot in the blazing heat from the hall on the long march to the cemetery.

I stayed in Sri Lanka until after the Christmas period. One of the difficult things for me was the fact that at all the meetings and gatherings I attended there was an empty chair by my side (where Railton should have been). We spent Christmas in Colombo as a family, but SO missed him. After this Janet and Derek returned to Pakistan, and Christopher and I returned to England.

Interlude II. England, 1988-1993

Life was very difficult for me during the first few months after coming back to England. There were times when I felt I could not and did not want to continue living. Death is so final and I felt as if I had been cheated out of my future. Margit, my Dad's second wife, who brought him so much happiness and extended his life by several important years, was very kind and understanding. But my Dad himself really did not help with his remarks as to how he saw the future for me. He informed me that: 'The Army never knows what to do with active and widowed Lt Colonels. I'm not sure what they will do with you, because you are a bit of an embarrassment all round.' He meant well, but his words – however much the fruit of experience – still hurt.

Christopher, who was now studying for a doctorate at Oxford, was very important to me at this time and always encouraged me to 'keep going.' He accompanied me to London for my first working day at my new job at IHQ. I had never been to London on my own and the whole journey was a turmoil for me. The old joke about the man who enquired of the receptionist at IHQ as to how many people worked in the building and the answer was 'only half of them' had long been known in my family, and yet from the first day there I was aware that the folk there did work extremely hard and long. My appointment was to be on Small Projects for Overseas Territories in the Development Section of IHQ. Commissioner John Swinfen was my boss, and was both kind and understanding. I cannot say I enjoyed office work. I found it repetitive, uninspiring and generally boring. I also felt that I was no longer an Officer and that there were many around me who were very good office workers, but had not had the opportunity or the calling as an Officer. One day, at a time of intense boredom, I actually went through my diary counting the weeks I had left before retirement (it was 174) and was then ashamed at myself for wishing my time away.

Being a widow was not easy for me either. I heard people around me saying: 'Oh she's strong – she'll be OK – just give her a bit of time and she'll come through it.' At Croydon even old friends did not know what to say or do around me. Whether it was embarrassment or concern I never knew. I only knew that former good friends would cross the street rather than talk to me, and I did not like it. The one thing I did enjoy during this time was being invited to various Corps to speak about the work in India and Pakistan. And in the next few years I was away many weekends.

I also decided that not enough attention was given to folk who were coming home or going back to the South Asia mission field, so that, whenever it was known that this was happening, I arranged a special evening get together at my flat in Norbury. The invitation would go out – along with the news as to who was going or coming, and the understanding that everyone would bring a plate of food. Nearer the date I would just phone around, make sure who was coming and ask if their plate would be sweet or savoury. It usually worked very well with me providing just drink and salad to top things up. I was pleased and yet surprised at the numbers who came. My main room was quite large but often the numbers spilled over into the passage and bedroom of the flat! I do remember that on one occasion Dad and Margit came up from Bournemouth and were able to be with us, and that was the day we had six Commissioners in the house! My old Dad was completely flabbergasted, and said: 'How many more have you invited?' He was in his element! Looking back on these few years I realize that the people who had declared me to be 'strong' had no idea of how weak and vulnerable and alone I felt. And yet I did decide to reinvent myself and to try again to be the person God intended me to be.

When after six years Commissioner Chianghnuna asked me to go to Calcutta I was more than ready. Although applications for visas had been refused for teachers, nurses, and even Doctors in the preceding two years, my visa was granted in three weeks. I felt this was confirmation that I should go. I also felt very special to be allowed my visa. My Dad was then well over eighty-five years old, and I felt I needed the last word from him regarding my decision. I made a special visit to Margit and Dad's lovely flat in Bournemouth, and said to Dad: 'The Army have asked me to return to India.' His reply was: 'Well, you'll go won't you?' So I did! Both Janet and Christopher supported and encouraged the fact that I was going back to India. I think they both realized that I looked upon the country as my second home, and as my happiest years had been in the East it was sensible to return. So this was proven. I do feel that returning completed the cycle of loss and renewal – I met new Indian friends, young people particularly, who became very important to me, and this helped me in my feeling of healing and gave me the ability to carry on with my missionary service.

CHAPTER FIVE

KOLKATA: CITY OF JOY

1993-97

Behala: 1992-4

My appointment back in India was to Kolkata to be in charge of the girls' home at Behala. The home was a purpose built building on the outskirts of the city. It had been built in the 1920s and was a typical Colonial building – solid, purposeful and a little ugly! It was spread over two large compounds with central lawns and the dormitories and kitchens around the outside, built on a raised platform of cement. There were 120 girls from the age of 4 – 18 and mostly orphaned or of low income one parent families. The staff were all older than me – most having lived in the home all their lives, first as girls in the home and then taken on as staff. They were hard working and supported me in many ways. Within a month of my being there things started to change. **Captain Chhotka Hembrom and his wife Bibliana** were sent to me as second officers and were so helpful the whole time we worked together.

Chhotka's English was not good when he came to me, but he did try hard and very soon we understood each other well. Chhotka was good to be around. He was cheerful, very interested in life, and generally wanted to experience anything new. He was also enthusiastic about work, which was particularly good on days when we had problems and bad happenings. Hembrom's home was in the hill region in Bihar and he was of the Santhali Scheduled Tribe. After some time of our working together, he was chosen to go to Sri Lanka for the South Asia College for Officers but had no passport. When we tried to obtain one we were told that no Santhali had

ever been issued a passport before, and they had no precedence for this. After lots of form filling and arguments, he became the first Santhali to have a passport, and since then has travelled to South Africa. England, and America on Army business. He was officially my assistant officer, but whenever I had a problem with language or officialdom he would step forward and say: 'Leave this to me', and I was happy to do so, knowing that the problem would be solved.

I know that sometimes he would be explaining to folk that, as I was English, I did not understand, and could not be expected to understand the situation, but we usually got there and that was all that counted. Over the years, Hembrom has grown to be not only a first class Officer, but also a faithful and loyal friend. Wherever he goes he attracts attention and interest for the gospel and is always happy to give his testimony. Mary Budge, a dear friend from Tavistock, who travelled with me to India at one time, declared him to be 'a modern Saint Paul' and so he is.

Lieutenant Suchitra Nyak was also sent to the home within a month of me arriving and was appointed as one of the helpers. I quickly realised she was not at all well and wondered why. No information was given from THQ and I was just informed that she was 'sickly' and it was felt the best place for her was Behala. She was tall, stately and quite beautiful in her own special way. A very private person, she kept herself very much to herself. Several times I tried to find out more about her but felt she was too shy to share. With the passing of time I learned that she had been a married cadet whilst in the Training College but that her husband had died in College. When I asked the cause of death I was told: 'General weakness and sickness'. In India many people do die as the result of stomach bugs and dysentery and I took it for granted that was it. When I later learned that a baby born to them had also died my heart went out to Suchitra, as I realized what a sad time she had experienced. Within the next year she herself became sick and when I asked her what she thought it was she said: 'It is the same as my husband – it is the sickness of death.' I vividly remember sitting on her bed and feeling as if I had been punched in the stomach – realizing that the whole family had been affected by AIDS and that Suchitra would be the last one to die – in Behala Girls' Home! When I asked her if she knew that it was AIDS and if Territorial Headquarters knew she said: 'Oh, yes. That is why I was sent here to be with you.'

I then went from feeling sick to feeling very angry, both about what I believed to be the possible danger to the children, and about the fact that THQ had seen fit to deceive me, or at very least to keep me in the dark. We looked after Suchitra as best we could and were surprised when THQ appointed her into Kolkata to the Women's Hostel – asking me not to divulge to anyone the reason for her sickness. She was there only six weeks when she died. In many ways, I was pleased she was not in the home as the girls would have been even more affected by her death. As it was her, family from Orissa took upon themselves the responsibility of her passage home and her burial. Again it was a case of THQ shelving the responsibility and just walking away saying: 'We knew you would know how to deal with the situation.' I felt very let down and angry for quite a long time.

Bondona's mother had died in childbirth, and her father was a *rickshaw-wallah*. Because he could not leave her alone he used to carry her in the sling on his crossbar most of the day and then they would go home together at night. This worked when she was a baby, but not as she grew. When she came to us she was six but could not walk. Her hands and feet were of normal size, but her body was disfigured and undernourished. Within three months she was walking well – finding her way to the dining room and eating everything put in front of her.

Keka's mother was a maid in a family house and tried to look after her daughter in spite of the fact that Keka was sickly. The child was then diagnosed with nephritis and it became necessary for dialysis to be administered. Because a maid's salary would not permit this, a previous missionary had said the Army would be responsible for Keka's dialysis and that she could live in the Girl's Home. Over the years the Assemblies of God Hospital had arranged treatment for Keka and the various missionaries, including me, in charge of Behala had willingly paid the necessary funds in order to keep Keka alive. When I left Captain and Mrs Hembrom in charge I was worried (he was the first national officer to be given the appointment and did not have extra funds). 'Don't worry', he said, 'I have a plan'. He went to the hospital and explained that over the years different missionaries had paid the funds for dialysis but now that he was in charge this would not be possible. When they expressed doubt, he reminded them of the large amount paid over the years and suggested that the local paper would be interested to know the story. The hospital then decided that Keka's treatment could be free.

Rupali was early in the care of the Army – having lost her parents in a house fire. She was a bright, busy and loving little soul who, in general, enjoyed life. Her one ambition was to be trained as a nurse, and she often shared this ambition with me. Examinations were not easy for her and I well remember the day she heard that she had failed her 10th standard exams, and therefore could not think of starting her training. It was well known that Asha, the Matron at Behala, would berate

any 'failures' for not trying hard enough (not that his fact ever helped the situation). Asha came to me to demand that Rupali should leave the home and then said 'Either she goes or I go'. I have experienced occasions when I have felt divinely guided and this was one of those. 'She will go,' I said, 'I will pay for her to go to the Women's Hostel in Kolkata whilst we find a place for her in nursing training'. Of course Asha was annoyed that I had taken Rupali under my wing, and never made this threat about any other girl in the future. In the intense heat of Kolkata in April, Rupali and I visited four hospitals to try for admission for nursing training. When we finally got her into the American Mission Hospital I felt at the end of my tether. 'When we get home,' said Rupali, 'I will wash your feet' – and she did! There is no doubt that she had to work very hard and long at the Mission Hospital. She received very little money but was so intent on finishing her service there. She has married a fine young man called Rajesh, who has a taxi service. They now live in their own house and Rupali works in the theatre unit of a specialist kidney hospital in Kolkata. I am proud to look upon her as my Indian daughter.

Polly was brought to Behala by her old grandpa. She was sassy, bright, innovative and at times annoying. When we had dramas or dances she always took the lead and did excellently. She too wanted to do nursing. I managed to enrol her with a lady doctor who used to mentor orphan girls for nursing. I was at this time retiring and leaving Kolkata and thought this was a good idea. When I returned 1 year later it was to find Polly thin and undernourished as well as desperately unhappy. When I asked to see her room she showed me to the general waiting room of the small hospital where the patients came during the day. All her personal goods were in one tin trunk which was pushed under one of the forms. Every evening Polly had to make her bed on the form and then sleep there, only to get up the next morning early in time to sweep and wash the room ready for the visitors. That was her accommodation. Three times during my stay in Kolkata, I made appointments to see Polly's mentor Doctor but every time she was 'too busy to see me.' Polly eventually found herself a job, and a husband; and though her husband has recently died, Polly now has her own flat in Sealdah, as well as a new job, and their son, Ronaljoy, is now a tall, bright teenager.

Sudha was a very beautiful girl from a Muslim family. She had three older brothers who had brought her to the home saying that they wanted her to be in our care until they were old enough to look after her. She had a mind of her own, and in many ways was stubborn. However, she was popular and would often look after younger children and protect them from 'bullies' around the home. When Christopher visited annually she would be happy to play chess with him and very often beat him! Her brothers did come and take her home when she was about 17, and although married early, she seems to have made a good marriage.

Aroti was one of the staff members in the home. She had been resident from the age of nine having been brought to the home by her elder brothers. They had been orphaned and promised that when they were older they would return to the home and look after Aroti. One day whilst at school she had fallen and cut her hand and, as a result, tetanus had set in. She had the usual face twisting and the Salvation Army had paid for to have a serious operation to correct this abnormality – but the operation was not successful. This left Aroti with a mouth which was considerably contorted and she was from then onwards unable to eat in public, having to eat only pulped food. When her brothers returned to take her home, they decided that they would not be able to marry her like that and so left her at the home! The rejection of that day must have been a life-long memory of horror. In spite of this she was a happy soul and worked for very many years as *khansama* (cook) in the home, and for the various missionaries who came and went. Her cooking was excellent and I looked upon her as a personal friend. I felt she was one of the people whom God had put in my path as an encourager. Two weeks after my visit for my 80th birthday, Aroti was cooking in her room and her nylon sari caught fire in the primus stove she was using. She was horribly burned and died just three days later bringing an end to her sad and yet fruitful life. I thank God for the memory of her.

During my time at Behala I was able to completely redecorate the whole compound. It had been neglected and was in dire need of an up-date. The money was available at THQ, but the officer before me had not wanted the 'trouble' of moving furniture and beds etc., that a redecoration would bring! I relished it and was so glad to see the big difference it made to the whole place. The rooves had been leaking and the resultant leaks in the dormitories had made the walls black and horrible. The new repairs and fresh paint made it such a joy to see and live in and the girls and staff were proud to show their friends and families around. One of the 'extras' I was able to enjoy was the fact that various young people from USA, New Zealand, and the UK came to stay and help at Behala. This meant that they were able to stay in the home and use it as a base whilst they went on their way as far as touring was concerned, but they also stayed to help in many ways. The first one came at a time of emergency as far as we were concerned. Out of the 120 girls then resident at Behala, 38 had hepatitis – and the problem was that we did not know until so many of them were ill. I therefore decided to put a notice in the Red Shield hostel in the city to say that I needed a nurse to come for at least two weeks, and would provide board and lodging. I also stated the problem with the sickness and said that barrier nursing would be necessary.

Andrea volunteered and came to us to work. She was a fully qualified nurse and was really the answer to my prayers. Instead of the two weeks she stayed six months and was most helpful in so many ways. She was on her way round the world and I think she needed a rest from constant travelling – and we provided that for her. She was from New Zealand and the third day, after the morning prayers she approached me and asked if she could have a typed copy of the Lord's Prayer (this was repeated every morning during prayers). This quite surprised to me as I thought she would already know this. She then explained that she had been brought up on a sheep station out in the country, her parents had no time for religion and had never been taught the Lord's Prayer. It had not occurred to me that I would be travelling all the way to India in order to witness to a young New Zealander about God's blessing in my life. When Andrea left Calcutta she travelled on to England and worked in a London Hospital for a few years before returning home.

Andrew, a friend of Christopher's from Oxford, who had also set up the Riverside Arts Project in Tavistock with Christopher and others, came to stay, initially for just a few weeks. He stayed far longer and really got stuck into the work and life of the home. He dug drains, cleaned out gullies, and did a great deal of physical work around the compound. He also felt that Aroti was special and she thought he was wonderful because he was able to repair a little cottage in the grounds which she had had her heart set on for a while. He was also good at drama and although his Bengali was non-existent and the girls' English was not good, they seemed to fully understand each other and I would often hear gales of laughter from the main room where Andrew was performing – or getting them to perform. He was good at building up the confidence of the girls and the general feeling of freedom in the home was good to experience. At Christmas there was a competition for a song amongst the churches which we entered. We all practised for weeks to make sure it was well done and we all felt sure we had a good chance of winning. I remember Andrew being so very upset when we did not win, and he wanted to complain to the powers that be for he felt it was obvious that we were the best!! We learned afterwards that the Cathedral choir always won – and, of course, they were the ones that won that year too! At the end of the school year, Andrew paid for the big girls (12 and over) to accompany him to the local restaurant for a *masala dosai*. They were thrilled and spent most of the day getting ready for the treat. I remember him stating that it was 'like flying with a flock of tropical birds' as they went along the main street as they were all wearing their best saris and clothes! Andrew has since become an excellent and successful writer – and one of his novels in particular, *TRASH*, owes a great deal to the transforming experiences he had during his time in Behala.

Christa was originally from the USA and had been working with Mother Theresa in Kolkata. The night before she was due to fly home, she was mugged and her passport and money were stolen. The US Embassy phoned and asked that she should stay with us whilst her new passport and fare home could be arranged. She came for a few days and stayed a few months. She was particularly good with the very young girls we had in the home (some were as young as four years old), and she spent a great deal of time with them teaching them action songs and telling them stories. They adored her and would sit in a circle around her and look up into her face and hold her hand in turn – thinking themselves special for that moment. Christa was important to us, but I like to think that we too helped her over an important time in her young life. She returned to America, qualified as a Doctor, and is now working in a deprived area in Southern California.

Towards what turned out to be almost the end of my time at Behala, my visa ran out, and I had to apply for a new one. My application was refused, and the Matron suggested that on my next visit to the visa office, I take some girls from the home with me to demonstrate why I needed to stay. Twelve girls of all ages dressed up and looking beautiful accompanied me on my next visit to a very surprised official, who nonetheless insisted I had to leave the country. He did, however, suggest that I went to Dhaka, in Bangladesh rather than all the way back to London, and he also provided me with a letter for the High Commission in Dhaka to plead my cause. At the time, Christopher had come to visit with **Deana**, his wonderful Irish girlfriend (and later partner). It was agreed that I would head across the border to Bangladesh, in the hope that I would be gone too long; Christopher set off on a long-planned train trip down to see the temples of Puri and Konark; and Deana was left in charge of Behala!

Kolkata Headquarters: 1994-6

I was appointed to be the **Divisional Commander of the Kolkata Division in 1994**, and was informed it was 'as a temporary measure'. This was quite an unusual and surprising appointment for me, and the fact that I was leaving the Girls' Home was not easy. However, Hembrom and his wife had been appointed as my successors there, and I knew they would do a good job. I was to live in DHQ at Kolkata, where we had lived as a family over twenty years earlier. But I was now alone, and my quarters was on the top floor, 167 steps up from the ground; in the hot months I was especially aware of this climb at the end of the day. Although no longer the centre of the India Northern Territory (the THQ had moved to Delhi), the Division was a large one with many Corps and Social Institutions. I felt the most important thing was to travel to the various places and visit the officers and get to know them and their problems. The last Divisional Commander was a competent man but was more interested in studying for his next degree than in caring for his officers and as I had voiced my opinion to the powers that be I think they thought my appointment might quieten me! I took real pleasure in visiting the outlying areas of the Division that had not been visited for years. The travelling was long, hard and uncomfortable but I always revelled in the faithful officers who were so glad to meet and greet me and show me their work and congregations. Now in my late retirement I am aware that many of the aches and pains I experience from day to day probably stem from the difficult travelling I did in those days – but it was all worthwhile.

An especially important visit I made during this time was to Hembrom's 'home', the Boys' Home at Simultala, to witness his work both in the Home and in the surrounding area, situated in Bihar – one of the poorest states in India. There was very little in the way of industry in the area and the ground there was dry barren and unworked. Small dry trees sprouted from the brown earth looking very forlorn and pathetic and the women dug the hard earth with very little to show for their efforts. The journey there was eight hours in the train from Howrah Station in Kolkata. It was not a main line train so I found it interesting to stop at so many small places. However, when we were about half an hour from our destination, Captain Hembrom casually mentioned to me that the train did not stop at Simultala, but he would give me good notice when the station came, and

then we would jump out! He said: 'Nothing to worry about as it does slow down. If we don't get off here the next station is 50 miles further on and the journey is not good.' I was scared stiff but decided I would try to 'go with it'. As we came into the tiny station, Hembrom turned to me and said: 'I will throw out our cases and then you must jump'. Out went the cases, and then he said: 'JUMP NOW, MRS WILLIAMS'...

I jumped and rolled down the grass bank and decided that it was not too bad after all – not half as bad as I had imagined during the past twenty minutes. When I was able to stand up and brush myself off I realized there was a special jeep for us. I was driven through the narrow streets of Simultala. 'Please stand up and wave to the people – many of them have never seen a white person before – and they will attend this evening's meeting if they see you,' said the Captain. So as well as having been scared stiff and shaken up considerably, I was asked to smile and look happy! My visit was wonderful and memorable and apart from having bruises on my hips for a few days, I survived to tell the tale and find a title for this book! I also lost my heart to the young boys in the Simultala Boys' Home, and over the next fifteen years funded eight boys a year and paid for furnishing from the proceeds of Bookworm Alley (of which more, later).

Colonel John Nelson (Secretary for South Asia) had discussed with me the possibility of appointing a new position within the All India structure. This person would need to be able to liaise with the existing Territorial Commanders and the Territorial Leaders in trying to bring forward the importance of the Social work in India, and also try to gain funding from various interested Territories and people around the world in order to fund new and better Social work. They would also need to travel extensively and conduct various Territorial seminars from time to time. I entirely agreed with him and said that I felt the Social work in India was important and wonderful, but very underfunded, and definitely 'at the bottom of the list' as far as Territorial Commanders were concerned. They seemed to be far more interested in building a new hall in the middle of nowhere than building a new dormitory in an existing overcrowded children's home.

In the spring of 1995 my homeland furlough was due, but before I returned home to England, Colonel Nelson asked me to consider becoming the new **All India Executive Social Secretary**. I was rather over-awed by this and felt that I could manage the 'personnel' bit of the job in visiting and doing seminars but was not so good at office management. During my consideration of my next appointment I was told of a certain Avril Porter from Ireland, the mother of a good friend of Christopher's girlfriend, who for years had wanted to visit India but now felt it was too late, as she was in her 50s.

To cut a long story short, two months after our conversation on the telephone, Avril paid her own fare to Kolkata and planned and completed my office work space. We entered a large empty room and within three weeks we had a beautiful (dark blue, light blue and silver) room together with a telephone, computers and office furniture. For my part I offered her board and lodging and an opportunity to be a tourist for one day of every week (usually taking her on my journeys). Over the next two years until my retirement she visited me every year in Kolkata, and then for 12 years into my retirement she travelled the length and breadth of India with me, always funding herself and donating significant amounts to various places we visited. Avril is a real and true friend to whom I am for ever grateful. In those days it was still not the done thing for single ladies to travel alone and the fact that she was with me was so important. At the end of the day we would laugh (and often cry) at the things we had experienced during our visits and the very catharsis of talking together made the work easier for me.

In Kolkata there was a large Social Services Centre housing over 400 workers, students and others; among these was a fine figure of man from Nepal, who goes by the unlikely name of **Dolphin.** He was at that time working for an international company, was clearly very ambitious and bright, and going places in the world. The officer in charge of the Centre repeatedly suggested that Dolphin attend the meetings at the Corps, and when he finally did so, he found himself very challenged both about his lifestyle and his future ambitions. Soon after this, he was invited to take part in some Army social work, and this led both to his calling and to our working together. He helped to set up a 'wrap-around' project with street children, who came to the Army for a meal in the morning before being given their uniforms to attend the local school; at the end of the day they would return to us for a further meal, leave off their uniforms and go back on the street for the night. In time there were forty children in this group, and Dolphin took on sole responsibility for this work when I left India to retire in 1997. It was after this time, in 2001, that he met Ailie, through a Christian chatroom on the web; in 2006, he moved to Holland, where they married. Through their Dutch church they now fund eleven pastors in Nepal, and also support thirty-six widows as well as a scheme which helps prisoners through rehabilitation. During our time in Kolkata, Dolphin became a valued friend; we are still in regular contact, and I am grateful to have come to know him.

Towards the end of 1995 Commissioner Nelson informed me that a **Lt Colonel Joyce Ellery** would be coming to India in order to visit a number of children's' homes throughout the country and that I was to accompany her. She had never been to India but was well known and highly respected in her own Territory of Canada and now, in retirement was to give India the benefit of her experience. I realised that we had already met whilst in Pakistan, for she had visited the territory in order to make a report on the various aspects of social work there. One of her particular interests had been the 'Goat Programme' in Khanewal, where Janet and Derek were working. This was a programme where a she goat and a male goat were gifted, by the Salvation Army, to a family and then, when the first baby goat came along the young goat was given back to the Army for further redistribution. The programme had commenced with just a few goats and was now in full swing with many baby goats being allocated every month to new families, amidst much rejoicing!! (Suffice to say that she was very impressed by the programme and was able to give funding for it when she returned to Canada.) As Joyce and I travelled on the long road from Lahore to Khanewal, we spoke of various Army people we had known over the years, and the Colonel mentioned a 'wonderful old retired English officer.' This man had visited his married daughter, who now lived in Toronto, and he had attended the retired officers' 'get together'. She was the guest speaker that day and they had sat on the same table and enjoyed each other's company very much. In the middle of the conversation I suddenly realised she was talking about my Dad and when I mentioned his name she was quite amazed. This, then, was the person coming to visit India and we would again enjoy each other's company as we travelled miles together during the next few months.

We visited four of the six territories in India in the two months she stayed, and as we went around I was aware of the fact the homes we visited and the sights she witnessed were very different to those she had experienced in her own land. Looking back, I realise that there was never a demeaning remark or a derogatory comment about the condition of our homes or the lack of training of our staff. She looked at the spirit in which this service was given and decided that 'our hearts were in the right place' and that the children were being looked after by people who loved them and cared for them in spite of the adverse circumstances in which they worked. She did report back to Commissioner Nelson that she felt more training could be given to the staff and that definitely more should be spent on the upkeep of our properties. The various Territorial Commanders had been very loath to spend money in this way and had always stated that our way of doing things was 'as good if not better than that of other churches.' This was not really the point – we had set our sights very low and now, after Colonel Ellery's visit, a new vision was presented to the leaders. Over the next few years the Colonel visited India several times and there is no doubt that her visits gave an uplift to our Social Services throughout the country. I feel that she was another special friend who came to India for this specific purpose, and I and so many others are grateful to her.

During one of her visits we travelled to Kolasib in the Indian Eastern Territory in the hills of Mizoram (above Bangladesh), in order to visit the Boys' Home there. While there, we noticed one boy who was obviously older than the other children and asked about him. He had been brought up at first at the Motherless Baby Home in Aizawl and later here in Kolasib, but always in the care of the Army since he was a small child. The Officers at the home said he was in special need, as it was time for him to leave the home but he had nowhere to go. Many of the children in our homes had an aunt or uncle or even old brother or sister who would be happy to accept them once their basic education was completed. This was not so with **Zohmingaiha**. So the officers were allowing him to stay until the Army made some decision regarding his future. Colonel Ellery said that it would be a good idea if I could get special sponsorship training for him, as he was obviously bright and attentive.

When I returned to Kolkata I made a request for sponsorship from England, America, Canada, and

Germany but no one was interested in a 17-year old: they all wanted younger children. Finally, I decided that I would try to fund him myself and, with the help of Avril Porter, this I did. Zoa (as he is known) travelled down from Kolasib to Kolkata – a journey of three nights and two days on his own – having never been out or his own area before. I admired his determination for it must have been a bewildering and even frightening time for him. Whilst in Kolkata we tried, with great difficulty, to communicate and to get to know each other. After the Easter holiday he returned to Kolasib and I promised to visit at the end of the school year and settle him in a college. Suffice to say that over the years he has studied hard and kept the high ambition to become an Indian Government worker. This has meant numerous examinations which, many times, I had doubts about. He, however was quite determined, and has now achieved his ambition, and has an important position in the Mizoram

government administration. Zoa and his lovely and very clever wife Muani have three fine children, Gaius, Railton and Aviana, and I am proud to call him my Indian son.

Another person very important to me at this time was Captain (later to be Lt/Col) **Shamu Meitie**. As I went to my office every day I noticed this smart good looking officer reading the Times of India newspaper. Although his office was in Kolkata he was obviously not from the area and I judged him to be from Mizoram. He was in fact from Manipur but his home Territory was Mizoram. It was necessary for someone from that area to be stationed in Kolkata in order to meet visitors who came from overseas and to host them whilst the arrangements were made for their travelling visa etc., for Mizoram. However, his main job was to be responsible to go, once a month to collect the money from the Bank of India in Kolkata and transfer it through to the India Eastern Territory. This was an important but not time consuming appointment and although Shamu was always in his office he seemed rather bored. I requested that he be seconded to me for the time available and my office would pay half his salary. His Territorial Leaders readily agreed and the International Secretary in London also thought it a good idea. It was one of the best requests I have ever made!

During the remaining time I served in India Shamu, and his little wife Ngnani, took me to their hearts and more or less adopted me as their special responsibility. Whatever time of the day, or night, I arrived at Kolkata airport from my visiting other Territories he would be there to meet me and take me to my flat, where Ngnani would be with a meal and fresh flowers to greet me. Again I felt special. I had prayed for someone to be able to see to the finances within my job – this he did remarkably well. I had prayed for someone who could drive in the terrible traffic of Kolkata and around, this, after taking lessons and passing his driving test, he did. I had prayed for someone I could fully trust to listen but not divulge certain plans for the future. This he also did. He and his wife had prayed that somehow, he would be asked to work with me so prayers were answered all round. During our time together he studied and passed his B.Comm degree and learned, from Avril, how to use a computer. The last thing he did for me was to completely plan, book, and arrange travelling for all concerned to the All India Social Service Secretaries' Seminar in Chennai (then Madras). I was just two months before my retirement and I was not feeling at all well. He took over the full responsibility and we had a most helpful seminar with Dr Grace Murdock. The Social Secretaries were all most appreciative and, I believe, learned a great deal during those days. Some of them had travelled hundreds of miles to be at the venue but this was half of the excitement for them! Within a few years Major Meitie was appointed to be Financial Secretary in both Ghana and Zambia and served a good term in both Territories before returning to his homeland. I am proud to call Shamu and Ngnani my special friends.

CHAPTER SIX

BOOKWORM ALLEY
AND BEYOND

My retirement from Kolkata was arranged by Major Shamu Meitie. He pulled out all the stops out and we had a full Kolkata Central Hall for this. The Divisional Commander (Colonel P. Yohannan) was very much in evidence, but Shamu had arranged all things well, and we had a varied and representative programme. So many garlands were presented to me that I could not carry the weight of the flowers around my neck and had to continually put them on a chair by myside, and certainly could not see over the top of them. As I addressed the people for the last time, I looked out on a sea of faces I had known for so long. Old, young and so many in between but every face meant a memory or a happening in their life or mine. I was grateful to God for calling me to the mission field and allowing me to be here at this moment in time.

However, I was by now more than ready to go home and felt very tired and almost weak with exhaustion. The Army had, of course, booked my ticket on the usual economy rate seat and this I duly sat at. Ten minutes into the flight a young flight attendant came up – checked my name and said 'Please come with me – someone has upgraded your ticket and you will be in First Class from now onwards. You are also invited to be in the cabin with the Captain from now until Delhi and have your first meal there.' So, with all my bits and pieces (an Indian drum, boxes of India sweets and so many garlands), I went up to the Captain's cabin and so enjoyed my meal with him, being shown the various important building as we left Kolkata and came into Delhi. I have never been told who it was who made the upgrade for me, but I am very grateful for it meant I was able to enjoy and relax during that last special journey home as an active Officer. I was not at all well, and within eight days had collapsed and was seriously ill with pancreatitis. I now realize that if I stayed in Kolkata the folk there would not have had the medical expertise to help me, whereas in the Croydon Mayday Hospital they could help me – and did. I was in hospital for five weeks and it was a long haul, leaving me feeling extremely weak and unable to cope on my own. I therefore stayed in Croydon for a month for rehabilitation, and for a second retirement service at what had been our home corps in Croydon. I then travelled to Tavistock in order to start my retirement – how grateful I was to do that.

My friend, Major Dorothy Allan, who had been so faithful to me during my time at IHQ, and had stayed in regular contact throughout my final years of service in Kolkata, journeyed with me to start my new life in Tavistock. But within two days I was admitted into the Derriford Hospital in Plymouth with malaria! All through the years on the mission field, both Railton and I had religiously taken our malaria tablets, and whilst he would have periodic bouts during which he could be very sick, I had never suffered from the illness. I can only think that because I was low from my Croydon Hospital experience the malaria surfaced for the first time. I felt extremely ill and did wonder if I would recover. Every evening at 9.30 I had the shakes, and there would be Doctors and nurses to witness this 'happening', as many of them had never seen the effects of malaria. Dorothy stayed with me for a few weeks and helped very much in the daily routine of shopping and cooking. I will always be grateful for her friendship and very practical help at that time in my life. I had been so looking forward to coming back to England and starting my retirement, and now I seemed jinxed at every turn.

Well before retirement I was thinking and praying as to what I could do whilst in Tavistock, where I planned to spend my retirement in Railton's old family house, left to me by his father. I felt I needed something associated with the Salvation Army, but did not wish to have an official job such as running a Corps. I also knew there were many young people in India who could use financial help, even if I was not working there any longer. I thought of various fund-raising ideas: embroidery, a stall in the Tavistock Market, and general public speaking appointments. Then, one day, whilst sorting through Railton's Dad's books, I came across the book *Sergeant Major Do-Your-Best* by William Booth and remembered how much it had helped me in my early Officership. I looked up the book on the internet and found that it was £14.00 (in 1998) and it occurred to me that this was the area I should pursue. If these rare books were presented well and if the service given was good they would sell. I informed my friends that I intended to have a book store and if they had books they no longer required, or if they were looking for a particular book, I would like to be contacted. After two years of recovery, sorting and cataloguing the books, I asked that an insert be placed in the Salvationist regarding the new service which would be known as *Bookworm Alley*, and we were up and running!

The response was most encouraging and a few weeks later I began a 'pick-up' journey around England and Wales to friends who had books for me. One of the first requests I had was from the daughter of Mrs Colonel Ivy Mawby. I remember Mrs Mawby as a powerful and effective speaker. The daughter was looking for a book by her mother with the title *From My Desert Island*. This was a compilation of various talks Mrs Mawby had given at women's meetings over the years. The daughter explained that she herself now had two daughters, and the first had been given a copy of her grandmother's book upon her 18th birthday. The second daughter was now nearing her 18th and had asked if a copy of the same book was available to her. No copy of this book could be found. THQ had been contacted as had Trade Headquarters, and then someone had suggested she try Bookworm Alley. Yes, I had a copy, and was happy to send it to the daughter for the granddaughter, with the compliments of Bookworm Alley – for that is where the book should have been – and now is.

Over the next 20 years and more, family and friends have been most supportive and I am grateful to them all. Leslie Banks, a friend from Croydon days, kindly designed and produced my often admired web-site. My son-in-law hosts the programme through which sales are generated, and my friend Don Pyman supported me in so many ways in my understanding of the computer. Without their help I would not have been able to operate so easily and effectively as I did. In so many instances I have felt that Bookworm Alley is just an avenue through which books travel to their destination. They are so often donated and given, and then within a short time, are on their way to someone needing them. During the first year of operation, I was contacted by the family of an 87-year old man in a nursing home. For four years he had asked for *Crochets and Quavers* – the story of a young bandsman in the Salvation Army Young People's Band. No one in the family could find it and – again – someone had suggested Bookworm Alley. The request was received on 18th December, so the book was sent by express delivery. After Christmas I received a very appreciative letter saying: 'I just wish you could have seen the look on Dad's face when he opened his present. Thank you for making an old man very happy.'

A quavery voice came on the telephone one day to ask if I had an old song book with the words of the song: *Into a tent where a gypsy boy lay, /Dying alone at the close of the day.* An 84-year old lady had been asked to sing a solo in the old people's home where she lived, and wanted the words. I found it in the 1953 copy of the Song Book and duly sent her a copy. The next phone call from her was to say that she had sung her solo and had been asked to sing again – another satisfied customer!

Plymouth is only about 12 miles from Tavistock and over the years I have benefitted by receiving concertina music and memorabilia from folk there. One of the best concertina bands in the United Kingdom was in Plymouth, and certainly one of the last operative. From America came a request for any concertina tutorials regarding how to play an Army concertina. The family remembered that their grandfather used to play and they now wanted to learn themselves. Over the next two years, three tutorials were sent, together with two Salvation Army Tune Books. The family tell me that they have grown to a band of three concertinas, and players who regularly get together and play at family gatherings: 'We really are quite accomplished now, and are receiving other invitations from friends to play for them, too.'

I was offered copies of the German Articles of War by a retired officer and was a bit reluctant to store them (storage was always a problem) – but did anyway. Several months later, friends from my time at Lincoln Corps came for a holiday. Both came from long-standing Army families and were both active in the band and songsters. Over the years they had left the Army and gone to enjoy holidays in Germany, where they drank the famous beer with their new found friends. A few months before visiting me, they had returned to the Army and renewed their commitment as far as not drinking was concerned. On return to Germany on their annual holiday, they found it difficult, because of their limited German, to explain to their hosts why it was that they now were not drinking. I then remembered the German articles of War I had stored and gave them the copy, knowing that the next year they could show their hosts just how important this way of life was to them. This couple later phoned and told me that the Articles of War had fuelled several nights of detailed discussion with their friends. I was glad I had stored the seemingly unwanted forms in Bookworm Alley.

From Exeter University came a request by a student who had heard that I had a good selection of Christian books and could she come and see them? I said yes, of course, and agreed that she did not need to buy, but could to borrow for a period of three months, any of the books she chose. After three months she returned, took 18 more books and brought with her three other students who were interested. They were not studying the Salvation Army as such, but their interests were in Strong Women (of whom we had plenty in the Army!), Victorian Women missionaries, and Social change made by religious groups. I found this to be both interesting and challenging, and felt it to be another way Bookworm Alley was used.

In August of 2004 General Shaw Clifton visited the area in order to conduct the 100th Anniversary of the opening of the nearby Corps in Launceston. The Officer of the Corps, Major Leonard McKnight, asked if it was possible for the General and his accompanying Officers to billet with me. This meant that under my roof I had the General and his wife, the Divisional Commanders Major and Mrs Clifford, and Jean Bradbury, and the General's Secretary Major Gaudion. I had said to them all that they could browse the books in the library whenever they liked, and when I got up at 7 a.m. the next morning, the General was already there – very interested and encouraging about everything in Bookworm Alley! During our conversations, he suggested that I go to the Army Butlin's Holiday Camp (held every year at various sea-side towns in England). I had already thought about this, but did not know how to gain an entry there. I did know that every year a couple of thousand Salvationists gathered for one week enjoying various meetings and so on, and I had long wanted to go. I also felt that when folk saw my books they would buy well. When I later asked for a space for a stall at Butlin's, and explained that the General had suggested this himself, I was 'in'; for the following ten years I was able to enjoy both the fellowship and the spiritual blessings of the weeks spent there. Over the years I learned the kind of books which were popular, and I also realized that small Army mementos were quickly bought. I therefore prepared things like crosses, Salvation Army flags, and little people in cross-stitch Army colours, together with tapes, compact discs, and old programmes for Army events – all of which sold very well. From the second year onwards, many folk donated books and memorabilia to Bookworm Alley knowing that things they no longer wanted would be used wisely and well. During the fifth year of operation, I returned home from Butlin's to Tavistock with a fuller car then I had left with – having made £800 profit for the work in India during the week

From the third year, a then new-comer to the Army by the name of Mary Budge accompanied me, and looking back, I realise that the trips to Butlin's would not have been so enjoyable or profitable for Bookworm Alley without her help. During the Butlin's years Ann Luxton, Bernice Riley, and Christine Woods also helped me on the stall and I was grateful to have their company. There is no doubt that our collective presence at Butlin's made Bookworm Alley more well-known in Army circles, and I look back on those years with enjoyment and gratitude. It is true that often people came to the stall thinking they knew what they wanted but sadly lacking the information we needed to help them. I remember a lady saying that she was looking for a book about a missionary who had worked in Africa. She had been given this book as a prize in her home corps but had lost it. Her memory of it was a green small book but she did not know the name of the missionary or the title of the book. After three days of looking on the stall, we found her book. It had a red cover, was a large book, and was a story of a missionary in India! Hallelujah! All in the course of service!

In my eightieth year I felt the time was coming when I should give the running of Bookworm Alley to someone else. Books are heavy to carry and climbing up ladders in my library was not really a good idea. After a great deal of prayer, I approached Philip Hendy and his wife Janet and they (I think willingly) accepted the charge of taking it on. Philip has, for years, been interested in Army History, and I knew Janet well from the time when she had worked with my husband many years before in Pakistan. The arrangements were made for them to come for three days to Tavistock. The first day all the books were removed, in alphabetical order, into plastic boxes. The second day all the wooden shelves were dismantled and stored in the van. The third day all the memorabilia was stored away and we celebrated with a fish and chip supper to tell each other how well things had gone! All the contents of Bookworm Alley now reside at the house of Philip and Janet in Hadleigh, and I was asked to go and cut the ribbon at the re-opening there in July 2017. Of course I have missed the books; of course I still get up in the morning and look for my e-mails and letters asking for information or for guidance; but I know that it was

the right thing at the right time, and am grateful to Philip and Janet for their thoughtful handling of the whole business. Under their stewardship Bookworm Alley has not only maintained its impetus, but also grown and developed. Janet has become a good travelling companion in the strange journey of life, and has been out with me to India on more than one occasion now, most memorably for my 80th Birthday celebrations with all the family at Behala. My special joy is that Bookworm Alley continues to fund young people and a range of new educational projects in India, as well as elsewhere. These projects include a whole new Salvation Army school soon to open in Vangaichungpao, up in Manipur State, with funds partly generated by Philip's heroic sponsored walk along the Great Wall of China!

I mentioned Mary Budge before, and must say more about her now, for she has become not only a trusty coworker, but also a trusted and much-valued friend, both to me, and to our family. It was back in 2002 that a new person attended our service at Tavistock Corps, for no other reason than she somehow felt she should come. She came to the meeting – never having been to the Army before – and quickly found her place with us. From that day on Mary has been faithful to God and the Army as well as to me. For two years I had asked God for a special friend to share my everyday experiences and this she became. Major Joyce Holmes, who was then the

Officer at Tavistock Corps, soon encouraged her to become an adherent. Mary quickly became fully involved in Army activities and took on the motto of 'heart to God and hand to man' very much to be her own.

She soon became a uniformed Soldier and has accompanied me to many places and experiences within my Army service – even travelling to India with me. We enjoy each other's company a great deal, and although we are very different we work well together. She has become my dearest friend in retirement, and I look upon her as a definite answer to my prayers. I am grateful both to God and to her!

Three times in the past twenty plus years of retirement from the mission-field in the Indian sub-continent, I have taken over the leadership of the Corps at Tavistock. We have had some fine, dedicated and competent officers. Most of them have not stayed long enough to really pull the Corps round. We have also had some mediocre, disinterested officers whose only interest was their next holiday and their coming retirement! Some of these have stayed too long! Each time I have taken leadership, we have been at a very low ebb, and there has always been the possibility that we might fold as a Corps. I vividly recall being told by one DC that my task was to shepherd the remaining few of the flock into heaven. But even through the hard times, there was never any doubt that the face of the Corps and the good name of the Salvation Army was well known and respected not only in Tavistock but in villages around, and support for us has always been there. We have sometimes been down to just five in our meetings for weeks at a time but we have carried on. One couple who have been most faithful and encouraging over the years is John and Sandra Dryden, with John bringing his years of experience to us as our bandmaster, and Sandra bringing the freshness of new soldiership to our meetings. As I write, we now have an Officer of our own, Major Pamela Smith (one of the very best ones!) and we are growing and progressing as a Corps. Mainly because of her enthusiasm and obvious sincerity we are happy to follow and work together. I am so grateful that now, in my eighties I am able to attend and enjoy a service which is well planned, and where the gospel is well presented, and where people respond.

EPILOGUE

On 27th December 2018, together with Christopher, I travelled once again to Kolkata. We visited various Army social institutions in and around the city, as well as several friends' houses. The Officers we met were mostly young, enthusiastic, and hopeful about the future; they were a joy to get to know. We stayed briefly in the new Red Shield on Sudder St, built on the site of the hostel which we lived in back in the early 1970s, and for a few days in the Fairlawn Hotel, just opposite: an old favourite of mine, which after a rocky period, is flourishing again. We were also wonderfully cared for both by Rupali and Rajesh in their lovely home and by the staff at the Oberoi – where we particularly enjoyed special breakfasts. We visited many  different eateries, enjoying Punjabi, Mizo, Bengali, Gujarati, South Indian and Chinese food with friends and extended family, including those who have figured strongly in these pages: Avril Porter (and her son, Steven, on his first trip to Kolkata), Rupali and Rajesh, and both Chhotka Hembrom and Zoa, who travelled many miles especially to see us. Together, we sat on the pavement drinking chai and espresso coffee, or made our way through the crowded, crazy Kolkata streets. The memories of this visit will last, treasured and long.

I am grateful to have been able to return to Kolkata a full thirteen times since my retirement. It was during the 2018 trip that I started the concluding sections of this memoir, with the feeling that my travelling days were done. Now the book is finally on the way to the printers, the COVID pandemic has prevented me from returning this winter, but I still hold out some hope of celebrating some part of my 85th year in the city I love. Whatever the future holds, I testify again to the leading of God throughout my life, and am glad to say that I still know His presence from day to day. I thank Him for calling me and enabling me to work for Him. I have enjoyed it all. To Him be the glory.

ACKNOWLEDGMENTS

I began by saying that my two children were my pride and joy. Janet, following many years of service with the Army and with the Church in Pakistan returned to England when her children were young, but she and Derek have not stopped working for the Lord. For the last 20 years and more Janet has been teaching English amongst refugee women in Bristol, and also enabling faith conversations between Muslim and Christian women at grass-roots level. Christopher also went into teaching, research, and writing, continuing at Oxford after his studies. He is now a Professor of French Literature, and as well as writing books about exciting topics from pilgrims to monsters, and a number of plays, he has taught several generations of students over the past thirty years and more.

I started writing this book mainly for my family: for my children and my treasured grandchildren and great-grandchildren: Lydia, Sarah, Elsie Mae, TJ, Joel, Ezra, Amariyah, and Caleb. It has gone through many changes before taking its final form and reaching other readers, and a number of people need to be specially thanked for their part in its journey. Dr. Stephen Childs, my nephew, read a draft of the whole story; Ken, my brother-in-law, not only made valuable suggestions and comments on different sections, but also redesigned and copy-edited the whole book, giving it new life and impetus at a crucial stage; Christopher initiated this project and has helped me considerably in and through its many twists and turns.

Hallelujah!